D0742284

The Ethos of a Late-Modern Citizen

The Ethos of a Late-Modern Citizen

Stephen K. White

HARVARD UNIVERSITY PRESS

Cambridge, Massachusetts, and London, England · 2009

Library of Congress Cataloging-in-Publication Data

White, Stephen K.
    The ethos of a late-modern citizen / Stephen K. White.
        p.   cm.
    Includes bibliographical references and index.
    ISBN 978-0-674-03263-7
 1. Citizenship.   I. Title.
    JF801.W53 2009
    323.601—dc22   2008041568

To my sister,

Ellen White Stringer

Contents

Preface

A friend of mine is a youth librarian in a county library system in the southern part of the United States. Some time ago, she and another woman got together to try to figure out how more Hispanics, especially children, might be persuaded to use the public library. They suspected that Hispanics might have a general fear of visiting what is essentially a government institution and a particular reluctance to leave their children there for reading programs. They hit upon the idea of celebrations at the library organized around holiday themes such as Feliz Navidad and Dia de Los Muertos. The gatherings were to be for whole families; as part of the celebrations, the children would spend a portion of their time in an organized, bilingual story-time session. These events proved to be quite popular. Other branches became interested, and at least one of them showed a documentary film about the hardships of a family whose father crossed illegally into the United States.

All this was generated from the ground up with no official encouragement or funding and with no political visibility; in fact, the planners were concerned that the county board of supervisors might get wind of these activities and react negatively. Indeed, over the course of 2007, protests from non-Hispanic residents increased. By means of phone calls and e-mails, citizens complained about how these programs encourage illegal immigration and waste tax dollars. One incensed citizen called a board member after driving by the library and seeing the sign out front announcing the Dia de los Muertos celebration. This man was incensed that his tax money was being spent for signs in a foreign language. He ended his call with a question: "This *is* the United States, isn't it?"

How should we interpret this train of events and the varying dispositions that are evident in them? The initial ideas and efforts of the librarian are not formally political, but they are certainly related to the health of our public life in a society that is increasingly feeling the stress that comes with multiculturalism. Moreover, they are not adequately comprehended by the familiar liberal idea of tolerance; clearly they go beyond any simple attitude of merely letting-be. Rather they seem to show a creative, small-scale, presumptive generosity by a member of a dominant cultural group toward a minority cultural group that is often on the receiving end of hostility and resentment, both at a personal level and at various governmental levels.

This book might be thought of as providing an interpretive frame for such dispositions of generosity and hostility. It is, of course, not the only possible frame. But it is one that attempts to locate these dispositions in close proximity to significant currents within Western ethical and political thought. The most important point of contact occurs at the site of struggle over how the Western tradition should respond to the challenges a late-modern world thrusts on us. Part of an adequate response, I argue, lies in the cultivation of a distinctive ethos of generosity within late-modern citizenship. I say "part" because I am not trying to reduce contemporary democratic politics to the practice of presumptive generosity and the dampening of hostility and resentment toward certain constituencies; rather I am trying to illuminate why it makes good sense to allow a certain spirit, or ethos, to infuse our political stances.

Acknowledgments

The stimulus to strike out on this project emerged from the intellectual ferment generated by a conference organized around my previous book, *Sustaining Affirmation: The Strengths of Weak Ontology in Political Theory*, at Northwestern University in 2004. I am deeply indebted to Keith Topper and Dilip Gaonkar for organizing the conference under the auspices of the Center for Global Culture and Communication. Thanks also to the cosponsors of the meeting: the Departments of Communication Studies, Political Science, and Philosophy, as well as the Program in Critical Theory. The exchange of ideas begun by the conference continued as the papers were prepared for publication as a special issue of the journal *The Hedgehog Review* (Summer 2005). I am grateful to James Hunter, the Director of the Institute for Advanced Studies in Culture at University of Virginia that publishes that journal, and to Jennifer Geddes, its editor, for bringing the papers into print.

The Virginia Foundation for the Humanities provided generous support and a marvelous atmosphere for finishing up a draft of the manuscript during the fall of 2007. It was a pleasure to be associated with such a fine public institution. I am especially grateful to Ann White Spencer and Rob Vaughan.

I had the opportunity to present portions of the manuscript as papers to various groups of scholars. I would like to thank my hosts at the University of Stockholm, University of Maryland, University of North Carolina, Yale University, University of Pennsylvania, University of Swansea, University of Toronto, University of Virginia, the Graduate Center of City University of New York, University of California–San Diego, the Philosophy and Social Sciences Conference in Prague, and the Virginia Foundation for the Humanities. I am grateful to the participants in those meetings for their many comments. Special thanks is due to those who read parts of the manuscript and offered detailed, critical insight: C. Edwin Baker, Fonna Forman Barzilai, Sonu Bedi, Samuel Chambers, William Connolly, Eva Erman, Peter Euben, George Klosko, Nikolas Kompridis, John McGowan, Sofia Näsström, Andrew Norris, Magnus Reitberger, Melvin Rogers, Morton Schoolman, George Shulman, and Tracy Strong. James Lesher and Eleanor Rutledge kindly helped me understand better the meaning of *ethos* in classical Greek life.

Deep appreciation goes to those who read and commented on the manuscript as a whole: my colleague, Lawrie Balfour, Sharon Krause, and an anonymous reviewer for Harvard University Press. Other colleagues of mine at the University of Virginia shared some of their social scientific expertise with me regarding the phenomena of resentment and inequality: John Echeverri-Gent, Paul Friedman, Lynn Sanders, and Herman Schwartz. I am grateful as well to Andrew Douglas for his research assistance. I owe a special debt to Bonnie Honig, who not only read the book but also provided me with many pages of careful and perceptive insights. Finally, thanks are due to my editor, Michael Aronson, for his initial interest in the manuscript and his care in bringing it to the point of publication.

Portions of Chapters 1 and 5 appeared as "Ethos and Late-Modern Democracy," in *Democracy and Pluralism: The Political Thought of William E. Connolly,* ed. Alan Finlayson (London: Routledge, 2009). Chapter 2 is a revised version of "Reason and the Ethos of a Late-Modern Citizen," in *Contemporary Debates in Political Philosophy,* ed. John Christman and Thomas Christiano (Blackwell, forthcoming). An earlier version of Chapter 3 appeared as "After Critique: Affirming Subjectivity in Contemporary Political Theory," *European Journal of Political Theory* (April 2003): 209–226. A small portion of Chapter 4 appeared in "Weak Ontology: Genealogy and Critical Issues," in "Weak Ontologies," special issue, *Hedgehog Review* 7:2 (Summer 2005): 11–25. And an earlier version of Chapter 4 appeared as "Uncertain Constellations: Dignity, Equality, Respect and . . . ?" in *The New Pluralism,* ed. Morton Schoolman and David Campbell (Durham, N.C.: Duke University Press, 2008), pp. 143–166. I would like to thank the publishers for their permission to reprint these materials.

As always, it is the spirit of my family, especially Pat's, that sustains me.

The Ethos of a Late-Modern Citizen

1

Introduction

Democracies face novel challenges today, and the role of citizens must be at least partially reimagined if we are to face those challenges in an admirable fashion; that is, in a way that neither denies, in the name of tradition, the force of what is new, nor imagines that we can adequately confront it by rejecting wholesale the traditions of modern Western political thought. I want to offer an interpretation of our late-modern ethical-political condition and elucidate how a distinctive spirit—or, more specifically, "ethos"—of citizenship might be made part of an exemplary response to this condition. I will suggest that the late-modern challenges faced by Western democracies constitute a serious predicament. The word *predicament* is useful here because it can indicate deep and complex troubles, without also implying an unmitigated bleakness of prospects. In recent years, judgments of democratic bleakness have become increasingly frequent on the part of political theorists. I sometimes share this concern that the prospects for a renewal of democracy are dismal. But such a portmanteau judgment may also lead us to dismiss too quickly the subtle but significant role that certain dispositions and actions may have for the enhancement of democratic life.

In what follows, I use the less familiar term *ethos* instead of *spirit*. The close relation of the two is evident in the definition of the former provided by the *Oxford English Dictionary (OED)*: "The characteristic spirit, prevalent tone of sentiment, of a people or community." *Ethos* is an ancient Greek word, and it was used by Aristotle in his theory of rhetoric.[1] Today, it is used with increasing frequency by political theorists.[2] My usage in the present context takes off from this general trend, but I will be arguing in favor of a particular, substantive ethos.

Although *ethos* is being used more often today, this frequency is not always matched by clarity of meaning. Hence, I will start with a brief attempt

to provide some elucidation (Section I). Then I will lay out more specifically, first, why recourse to the idea of ethos helps us grasp our current
ethical-political challenges in a distinctive and valuable fashion; and, second, how each of the chapters advances this agenda (Section II).

I. What Is an Ethos?

The usage of *ethos* has been growing over perhaps the last twenty-five years or
so, at least since Michel Foucault's highly visible adoption of it in the early
1980s.[3] Given this lineage, it should not surprise anyone to find that recourse
to this term is typically entangled with critiques of core commitments of
modern Western thought. My efforts are in some degree of accord with this
emphasis, although I will be employing *ethos* to refer specifically to affirmative ways in which we can engage more reflectively the distinctive challenges
of late-modern life. The recourse to *ethos* is part of my overall attempt to re-
work some of the basic figures of our modern political imagination, including our conception of the self, our core moral concepts, such as human
dignity and respect, and our understanding of the character of citizenship
and the tenor of democratic politics. Starting from the terms of the *OED* definition, my goal might be described as trying to answer the question: What
sort of "characteristic spirit" or "sentiment" should we be trying to cultivate
as we seek to confront the deep challenges of late-modern life?

   A useful way to begin approaching this task is to consider some of the ways
in which *ethos* has been employed as part of strategies of contesting mainstream, modern expectations about practical reason and political conviction.
Consider a well-known usage of the term in an interview Foucault gave in
1983. The interviewer wanted to probe the question of whether Foucault's
later genealogies and writings on the self could be described as being only
about ethics, not politics. In response, Foucault tried to show that his work did
indeed resist notions of the ethical-political such as Jürgen Habermas's,
wherein one sees a political perspective as being directly derivable from a universalist, deontological understanding of what practical reason obligates us to
think and do. Against this sort of background, to think in terms of an ethos, or
"manner of being," implies skepticism of both universalizing neo-Kantian
reason and the idea that a substantive political position can be derived merely
from the application of that reason to a given historical situation.[4]

One might interpret Foucault here as grandly rejecting any role whatsoever for practical reason in public life and distancing himself from any systematic ethical-political perspective, on the grounds that such commitments inevitably serve agendas of domination. But one might also interpret Foucault in an alternative fashion: as issuing a challenge to later scholars to think about practical reason and our most basic political commitments somewhat differently. My efforts are animated by this second reading. But in this endeavor I do not feel bound to keep my response in line with what Foucault might have endorsed.

Keeping this broad perspective in mind, why do I refer to my response as distinctively "late-modern"? I do so to highlight two points. First, my response embraces philosophical insights that clearly depart from at least some familiar, modern ones. At the same time, however, it also denies itself some of the easy self-confidence or sense of unmitigated liberation from modern commitments that sometimes has accompanied responses identified as "postmodern." Postmodernists tend to view as deluded those who are still wedded to the conviction that their ethical-political commitments are securely grounded in some foundational "metanarrative."[5] The need that foundationalists feel for secure footing is, as Richard Rorty tells us, like an imaginary itch. You should simply cure yourself of that delusion rather than continue to scratch futilely.[6] Foundationalists typically reply to such tendentious characterizations with the equally tendentious countercharge that while postmodernists smugly congratulate themselves, they fail to notice that they are slipping into the abyss of nihilism.[7]

To embrace a late-modern ethos in my sense is to disallow oneself the comfort of *either* of these familiar put-downs. An individual with such an ethos will take seriously many of the insights that animate postmodernists; but whichever of these insights she is moved to embrace, she also knows they do not offer any truth that is capable of automatically trumping the foundationalist's convictions. Alternatively, my late-modern individual might be committed to some variant of theism; but if she is, she must also admit that there can be other ways of spiritually animating one's life that cannot summarily be dismissed as nihilistic.

Such views reflect the fact that my exemplary late-modern individual carries her most fundamental commitments in a "weak ontological" fashion. A weak ontology, as I have shown elsewhere, comprises a set of ontological figures of self, other, and the beyond human, as well as some basic conceptu-alizations of how those figures interrelate in terms of language, finitude, natal-ity, and the articulation of our deepest "sources of the self."[8] One's ontology in this sense is that to which one is most fundamentally committed. But the *depth of one's commitment* does not translate immediately into *absoluteness of conviction.* The meaning and significance of this claim will become clearer in Chapter 2 and succeeding chapters. For the moment, one only needs to un-derstand that an ethos is animated by a given set of ontological "figures." A constellation of such figures sustains an ethos in the sense of prefiguring its cognitive perspective, moral bearing, and aesthetic-affective sensibility. And that ethos, in turn, provides us with an orientation, or disposition, toward everyday life and the ethical and political problems we encounter there.[9]

In referring to Foucault, I just noted that his usage of ethos is often inter-preted as involving a critique of practical reason.[10] This suspicion seems to hold rather generally in relation to those who want to emphasize the impor-tance of the notion of ethos. And there may be some truth to this suspicion, at least in particular cases. Certainly the concept of ethos seems to be contin-ually employed in ways that are interwoven with concepts such as affect and identity that stand in apparent contrast with characteristics of reason such as dispassionateness, disinterestedness, and neutrality. Thus it is not surprising to find scholars referring to "a framing opposition between rationality and ethos."[11]

II. The Itinerary

My argument will be that an opposition between rationality and ethos is un-necessary. This point is important to establish clearly, because otherwise my subsequent claims risk being dismissed by some as just so much fashionable postmodern irrationalism.[12] To preempt such an objection, I will begin in Chapter 2 to explicate my idea of an ethos of late-modern citizenship in the context of its being a *reasonable* response to certain crucial challenges to modern Western political thought.

I am aware that all claims to reasonableness have significant drawbacks. Particularly problematic is how often appeals to such a standard tend to mask powerful interests. Additionally, even when a claim to being reasonable is deployed with the best motivations, this criterion always remains relatively imprecise. Despite these risks, I still think it is useful to describe the ethos I defend as involving a claim to reasonableness. For present purposes, I will refer to two senses of *the reasonable*. They are distinguishable in that they apply to different objects and embody somewhat different criteria. The first sense applies to persons whose behavior one wishes to influence in some action context. One advises or admonishes the other to: "Be reasonable."[13] When this phrase is used, the speaker typically intends to solicit an *attentiveness* to certain especially significant characteristics of the context of action and to appeal to a minimal sense of *moral self-restraint*. One way of characterizing this book is to see it as bringing to coherence an ethos that is oriented around the urging of citizens to be reasonable in how well they negotiate certain distinctive challenges emerging on the contemporary ethical-political landscape. Thus a late-modern ethos is at least partially structured by an exhortation to be especially attentive to those challenges and to show a certain self-restraint in engaging them—in pulling back from what might otherwise be the most probable initial reaction.

Part of the substance of this ethos resides in the particular ontological figures that animate its claim to reasonableness. For example, our basic sense of orientation to others reflects our underlying figuration of the self; that, in turn, stands in a relation of reciprocal constitution with values such as human dignity and respect. And all of this unfolds, finally, through a critical engagement with the Western tradition of ethical-political thought. This brings me to the second sense of reasonable to which I appeal. Here the object of evaluation is not in the first instance a specific course of action but rather the adequacy of a particular interpretation of a tradition. In relation to this claim, I draw upon Alessandro Ferrara's insightful work on the judgment of a given symbolic whole as "exemplary."[14] Accordingly, one can see my claim to be one of offering a *reasonable* or *exemplary* interpretation of, first, certain fundamentals of modern Western political thought; second, the character of the challenges late modernity brings to that tradition; and, third, what at least part of an appropriate response to those challenges looks like. Exemplarity, or reasonableness, in this second sense has to do with *how deftly and innovatively a tradition can be articulated in the face of challenges.* The goal is to project an exemplary *furtherance* of the life of that tradition: "to set," in Ferrara's words, our "imagination in motion and to produce the feeling of . . . [a] furthering of the range of possibilities" of our political life. This furtherance carries a validity that is neither merely internal to a particular tradition nor abstractly universal. Although this validity applies initially to what furthers the flourishing of a particular tradition, it also ultimately involves its possible ability to "exert a cogency outside of its original context."[15] I aim for this sort of validity in the congruence I develop between the tradition of Western political thought in the prosperous and secure democracies, on the one hand, and the ethos I offer as a response to the late-modern challenges that confront that tradition today, on the other. The force of exemplarity here thus extends to those whose task it is to attend to our future by imaginatively renewing our traditions in the light of novel, global challenges, as well as perhaps even to those in non-Western cultures engaging in analogous efforts.

The case for my ethos's being exemplary does not equate to a claim that it is exclusively so. Other *ethe* (the plural of *ethos*) that appeal to different aspects of the tradition of Western political thought can stake similar claims to being exemplary. For example, I take Charles Taylor to be elaborating a late-modern, theistic ethos in which the commitments within that tradition are judged to require our being tied to an animating *agape* that reproduces among humans God's love for creation.[16] Similarly, but nontheistically, Wendy Brown has argued for what I would categorize as an ethos of citizenship. She understands this attitude to involve more the cultivation of a certain disposition toward other community members rather than the derivation of a set of principles providing "an orientation toward law and the state." Here loyalty to one's community is understood as a "civic love" that expresses itself in a thoughtful, Socratic dissent, as well as in practices that vivify and resist the potentially destructive forms that such love can take—something especially pressing in an era of patriotism and terror.[17] The ethos I will articulate is, like Brown's, nontheistic, but its central orientation is captured less by love than by the virtues of attentiveness and a gratitude toward the *presencing* of being that we express in actions bearing witness to that character.[18] The specific sense of these claims will emerge over the course of the book.[19]

A critic might object that all such appeals to an ethos are unrelated to citizenship in a strict sense. That concept involves criteria of membership in a political order, as well as the rights and duties that follow from that status. One either formally belongs to that order or does not. This sort of objection might have carried some weight two decades ago, but it sounds almost quaint now. Citizenship has evolved from being a relatively simple, staid concept to being a highly contested and multidimensional one. Terms such as "differentiated," "multicultural," "hybrid," "transnational," and "world" citizen indicate an entanglement of the symbolic wholes toward which individuals orient themselves and feel some sense of public obligation. I am not going to address this tangle of issues directly, but rather simply locate my attention to a late-modern citizenship within this phenomenon of proliferation.

My concern with citizenship is also, as I noted previously, limited in the first instance to prosperous Western democracies with their relatively stable and, at times, quite admirable political traditions. This initially restricted spatial orientation will, however, open out onto expectations that we inhabitants of these societies face as conscripts of late-modern time and as participants in broader political wholes. We might compare our current situation to the one Denis Diderot and his *philosophe* friends confronted in the mid-eighteenth century. His thinking certainly reflected specific concerns he had as an inhabitant of a distinct and privileged place, namely, France. But just as important, if not more important, to him was his sense of being implicated in the challenges of a novel time that came to be called the Enlightenment. And these challenges were so vivid for Diderot that the symbolic whole of humanity began to decenter the privileged symbolic wholes of France and Europe. For Diderot, his obligation to enlightenment meant that he could no longer envision humanity as a subcategory in the imagination of European empire.[20]

Today, as we try to think creatively about the different symbolic wholes toward which we might orient ourselves, the notion of ethos helps to persistently draw our attention toward the aesthetic-affective dimension that is always involved in the dynamic process of fashioning our identity. Within the liberal tradition, citizenship has largely been a matter of the rational determination of one's obligation to obey the law. If aesthetic-affective issues were admitted to the determination at all, they tended to hover uncomfortably and incongruously in the background in the form of patriotic sentiments. Today, however, even many liberals are much more interested in the problem of the aesthetic-affective soil necessary to the flowering of central liberal virtues, such as self-restraint, moderation, and reasonableness.[21]

My overall argument in the book is structured as a series of responses to what I take to be the most significant challenges of late modernity. I specify the force of these challenges within five analytically distinguishable but overlapping spaces of reason giving on the contemporary ethical-political landscape. In relation to each of these spaces, my response will constitute a delineation of what we should expect from a reasonable actor in conforming to the previously announced criteria: moral attentiveness and self-restraint. The five spaces of practical reason are (1) where cooperation is sought involving the justice of basic social and political structures; (2) where reasons are articulated for affirming the "foundations" or "sources" of our ethical-political judgments and actions; (3) where insight is sought in the struggle for recognition of identity; (4) where we are called upon to expand our ethical-political imagination beyond the boundaries of the modern state to include claims to human rights and global justice on the part of distant "others"; and finally, (5) where we argue about the prospects of democracy. Within each of these five interrelated spaces, I will specify a corresponding core ethical disposition that is responsive to the respective challenge and animated by a particular set of ontological figures. The constellation of challenges, disposition, and supporting figures provides a minimal content in relation to which the expectations of attentiveness and self-restraint are oriented within the respective spaces. A late-modern ethos of citizenship accordingly displays its full character in the judgments and actions of individuals who sustain this fivefold set of expectations.

Chapter 2 elucidates further why the notion of the reasonable is given a prominent place in this project. There I also lay out the challenges that appear in the first three spaces of practical reason, as well as the corresponding senses of attentiveness and self-restraint that characterize a late-modern ethos's response to those challenges.

The notion of ethos that I am affirming also demands some elucidation of the broader conception of subjectivity or the self within which I envision this ethos being incorporated. The mainstream, modern conception of the self has been much in dispute in recent years. A good portion of what we associate with postmodernism or poststructuralism involves criticisms of this conception. Chapter 3 takes up this issue and assesses what is persuasive and what is not in these criticisms. The aim is to sketch subjectivity in a fashion that does justice to those critical concerns and yet also is robust enough to bear the weight of a late-modern ethos.

Chapter 4 continues the discussion of subjectivity in the context of questions about how well our Western ideal of the *capacious* subject allows our moral imagination to adapt to the global level of practical reason, where we are called upon to respond to the claims of distant others.[22] To imaginatively engage others on this site of practical reason, we would do well to revise the way we think about the core values of human dignity, equality, and respect, and how they are understood in relation to the figure of the capacious subject. I argue that the slender and fragile bond of humanity that those values trace is better imagined as taking shape not only from an understanding of ourselves as uniquely capacious creatures, but also from a refigured understanding of ourselves as finite, mortal ones. Although I will be speaking in this chapter primarily about the sort of geographical and cultural distance that has come into special vogue with the themes of globalization and multiculturalism, I would argue that the insights developed here about expanding moral imagination in relation to these sites are also useful when engaging other sorts of symbolic distance, such as economic, racial, and sexual.

Finally, in Chapter 5, I consider how the notions of subjectivity and ethos that I develop might help us begin to sketch a distinctive, democratic conception of citizenship. This conception needs to be elaborated in such a fashion that we can see its value for addressing the specific way in which our democratic ideas and institutions are challenged in late modernity. This challenge has three facets that together constitute our current democratic predicament. Moreover, the character of these facets is such that they make a renewal of the democratic spirit simultaneously pressing and difficult to conceptualize within the traditional terms of democratic theory. The first facet involves the rapid growth in economic inequality that makes increasingly tenuous any minimal sense of commonality and fairness that has always been taken to be crucial to a democratic, constitutional order. Second, the changed social composition of affluent, democratic societies renders the classical conceptualization of the shape and trajectory of democratic renewal rather problematic. By this I mean that it is increasingly difficult to imagine an emergent, robust *demos*—the ancient Greek term for the people in their sovereign political capacity—that is brought to life by igniting the latent, shared interests of those in society who constitute *both* the majority numerically and the most disadvantaged economically. That familiar notion of the demos depends upon the prior assumption that a society has the shape of a pyramid, with the poorest also being the most numerous. Affluent Western societies today, however, are typically shaped more like a diamond (with the bottom point ground down somewhat).[23] Thus the second facet of our late-modern predicament concerns the disappearance of the empirical referent for the classical ideal of the demos. The modified diamond shape implies that democratic majorities will have to be constructed at least somewhat differently, with more attention paid to at least some portions of the middle segment (that is, those located near the widest part of the diamond). Finally, the third facet of our democratic predicament concerns the growing readiness of contemporary political theorists to dispute the legitimacy of that classical ideal itself as the ground of democratic hopes. By this, I mean that the image of the sovereign, autonomous demos has continued to lose its status as the normative touchstone of democratic legitimacy. What implications follow from this disinvestment? More pointedly, what sort of alternative normative basis should we affirm when thinking about the revitalization of democracy?

The challenges of late modernity raise a host of difficult questions. It would be exceedingly presumptuous of me to claim that the late-modern notions of subjectivity and ethos I develop in the following pages provide anything like an adequate response to them. My claim, rather, is only that they provide better initial insight into these matters than other perspectives that promise us some guidance toward a democratic renewal.

2

Reason and Ethos

Through much of the history of Western political thought, an appeal to reason occupies a central role. In that appeal, there resides a conviction that an orientation to reason carries with it at least some sort of initial traction for our engagement with the most significant problems of political life. By *traction,* I do not mean merely an instrumental grip on problems in the sense of a rational strategy that promises to efficiently enhance my self-interest.[1] Rather, I also mean at least a minimal cognitive and dispositional grip in the sense of some orientation toward justice and general well-being. When one appeals to reason in this fuller sense, one has what I will call an *emphatic* conception of practical reason.[2]

In the history of Western political thought, this emphatic character was often represented by images of intense light and penetrating vision. Think of Plato's description of emerging from the cave into the light. Or think of the representations of Enlightenment ideals in the eighteenth century that show the sun penetrating through the rain clouds, bringing renewed warmth, clarity, and well-being to the town below.[3] Translated into moral-political terms, reason in this sense promises to reveal a clear foundation of universally valid values and principles that can slacken the propensity to social conflict and rise above the discordant particular claims of different traditions, classes, religions, and nationalities. Such emphatic conceptions of practical reason came in for increasingly intense criticism in the twentieth century. The most important line of critique for present purposes is the one stretching from Max Horkheimer and Theodor Adorno's *Dialectic of Enlightenment* in 1947, as well as Martin Heidegger's essays shortly after that, to the work of Michel Foucault and other poststructuralists beginning in the 1970s and continuing today.[4] At the most general level, these critics argue that those who have operated within the dominant spirit of the Enlightenment have failed to understand adequately a danger underlying the determined pursuit of freedom and happiness through reason. The confident pursuit of these ideals in the form of universalizing ideologies and techniques of human organization betrays an unacknowledged will to dominate. This will knows itself only as a benign desire to subdue nature and to reform the recalcitrant qualities of self and society, all in the name of an increasingly just and progressive way of life. A wholehearted adherence to this range of projects became all the more pressing as religion was increasingly pushed toward the margins of modern life. The loss of Christianity's promise of immortal life had to be compensated for by the promise of an unending expansion of human capacities and well-being. The anxiety of finitude was thus displaced by a will to dominate that increasingly brought with it what one might call a sense of immanent infinitude. Edmund Burke was perhaps the first to perceive this phenomenon. He saw it taking shape in the French Revolution. Even before the period of the Terror, when rooting out enemies of the revolution became an unending task for true patriots such as Robespierre, Burke saw in the great revolutionary festivals a new sense of the infinitude of human will and reason.[5]

Curiously enough, then, it is a conservative who first develops the key insight out of which radical critics of the twentieth century launch their arguments. The claim is that entangled with the admirable ideals of enlightened Western life is an unbounded and unacknowledged willfulness. Divine Providence has been replaced by a mode of reason that embodies "an attentive 'malevolence' that turns everything to account."[6] It is only after we have fully embraced the world as standing completely open to our projects that we can—with the best of intentions—find ourselves simultaneously pursuing emphatic notions of reason and freedom and persistently expanding the reach of what Foucault famously calls "disciplinary power" and "normalization."[7]

Thus for twentieth-century critics of modernity, attempts to reason toward justice and common good that style themselves as anything like the beneficent spreading of light into darkness are deeply deficient. Although Foucault, as well as Horkheimer and Adorno, often spoke as if this deficiency extended to every possible variant of emphatic practical reason, they should not be taken at their most hyperbolic word. In each case, evidence suggests that they did not so much condemn emphatic reason per se, as they counseled far more caution and self-reflection in our appeals to reason.[8] We always retain at least some capacity to develop dispositions and practices that persistently chasten reason's overreaching promise to reconcile with finality the different voices of humankind.

The aim of this chapter is to begin to sketch what such an appeal to a chastened but still emphatic notion of practical reason might look like and what sort of core normative disposition, or ethos, we might affirm as appropriate to a reason that bears this late-modern burden. I refer to such a chastened appeal and minimal orientation as expressing the qualities of reasonableness. Let me emphasize again that I use this notion in two senses. One refers directly to the degree of *cogency of the interpretations* I develop regarding the challenges with which late modernity confronts our traditions of Western political thought. A key concern here will be how adequately these interpretations and the insights developed from them help us to craft strategies for slackening an insufficiently acknowledged will to dominate within that tradition. The cogency of interpretations in this sense opens into the second sense of reasonableness that applies more directly to the orientation of an individual's course of action. When I advise, or admonish, you in this sense, I urge a kind of *moral attentiveness* and *self-restraint* that you should display in relation to the clashing voices that engage one another in contemporary political life. As I indicated in the Introduction, I want to elaborate a late-modern ethos that has the capacity to provide us with an exemplary, or reasonable, orientation within five spaces of practical reason-giving. This ethos is exemplary insofar as it responds innovatively to the challenges late modernity presents to us, while maintaining a significant attachment to the tradition of Western political thought. Citizens who manifest such a late-modern ethos of citizenship possess a robust resource that can be drawn upon for orientation as they engage the institutions, practices, and competing faiths of contemporary political life.

This chapter considers late-modern challenges within three of the five spaces, or sites, of reason-giving. Each of the three sections of this chapter corresponds to one of these sites. Section I considers the site upon which one seeks possible grounds for cooperation involving the basic fairness of social and political structures. A major reason for starting here is that Rawls's efforts on this terrain can function both as an aid and as a foil for my own. In *Political Liberalism,* he proposes an exemplary way of construing what it means to be reasonable in this space and how that orientation constitutes a

central component of a late-modern account of justice.[9] Rawls calls his principles "political" in that they can be agreed to in a fashion that is "freestanding" in relation to foundational philosophical or religious views.[10] This
strategy of argument makes good sense generally, but I want to draw attention to one way in which his account is in fact more dependent on foundational commitments than he admits. By this I mean that his criteria for what
it means for a person to be reasonable are quite strong; and, as others have
persuasively argued, the only way he can justify so strong a definition is
through a tacit affirmation of the foundational moral idea of equal respect
and a corresponding ontology that constitutes persons as entities having dignity and thus being worthy of respect.

My intention in calling attention to this foundational element in Rawls is
not to contest directly the validity of his theory of justice. Rather, it is to help
isolate one of the central moral-ontological constellations within which a
persuasive notion of a late-modern reasonableness can take shape. Another
way of saying this is that Rawls may not be obliged to worry about implicit
foundational issues, given his specific goal of constructing a political conception of justice, but I am, given my task of providing a sense to the idea of an
ethos that reflects more broadly on the relation of reason and politics today.

Sections II and III pursue this task further by teasing out what it might
mean to be reasonable in relation to two additional sites. In Section II, I consider more directly the site where we, as late-moderns, articulate the central
ontological figures that provide the foundations, or sources, of our core normative claims in ethics and politics. In Section III, I turn to what is often
called the struggle for recognition of identity. This third site is somewhat different from the first two which have traditionally been at the center of political reflection in the West. What is different today is exactly how we orient
ourselves on these sites. But the very existence of the third site is, to a significant extent, an artifact of late-modern times.[11]

My overall intention is to elucidate how the claim to reasonableness
would draw us to be attentive and exercise self-restraint at each of these
three sites. The criteria of attentiveness and restraint operate differently at
each site; but the claim to reasonableness at one site is constitutively entangled with the corresponding claim to reasonableness at the other two. I will
expand this picture in later chapters, adding two more sites: where we are
called to expand the scope of our moral imagination to distant others, and

where we are called to orient ourselves to the challenges of democracy's current predicament. One whose action embodies such a full, fivefold claim can be said to manifest what an emphatic but chastened reason might mean for a late-modern citizen.

I. Site One: The Terms of Cooperation

Rawls's *Political Liberalism* is a justly famous effort to sketch out the implications of appealing to "reasonable" individuals for the purpose of constructing a theory of justice. He understands this appeal to reason as one that (in my terms) is chastened but still emphatic. It is chastened by a primary insight, or lesson to be learned, from the history of modern Western political life: that the clashes between different conceptions of the good show no signs of being definitively resolved in favor of any one of them; and, accordingly, we must take account of this underlying "fact of reasonable pluralism" when we reflect upon political life today.[12] A failure to accept this fact leaves a society open to political domination by one group or another claiming the right to enforce its view of the good. A theory of justice that rejects this kind of claim must configure itself in such a way that it remains, as I previously noted, freestanding in relation to any particular foundational or, in Rawls's words, "comprehensive" moral or political view. Rawls's theory is thus chastened in that it disallows appeals to reason that claim to be capable of peering through and fully resolving differences between alternative foundational claims. Such a theory of justice finds its basis of agreement at the level of an "overlapping consensus" between adherents to different, but reasonable, comprehensive views of the good.[13]

If this is the way Rawls interprets reason's being chastened, how does he interpret its being emphatic? This is apparent in the normative and dispositional content he assigns to being reasonable. Being "reasonable" means that one is willing "to propose fair terms of cooperation and to abide by them provided others do." One is to be attentive to a standard of fairness between competing claims; and to restrain oneself so as to affirm and seek agreement on only those political arrangements that embody such a standard. In the same spirit, one restrains any propensity for intolerance of comprehensive doctrines one might dislike, as long as they can plausibly be seen as within the bounds of reasonable pluralism.[14]

For the most part, Rawls's interpretation of attentiveness and restraint in relation to the matter of the justice of basic structures seems to me to make good sense. It also makes good sense for him to seek to make his account of justice as freestanding as he can. But, as I indicated earlier, it is not entirely freestanding. Charles Larmore has made this point quite clearly.[15] He contends that Rawls's notion of reasonable agents who are willing to seek and abide by fair terms of cooperation tacitly builds into his account an "underlying view of human dignity and of the respect we thereby owe each other and every human being."[16] In other words, it is only individuals already embracing this disposition of equal respect who will be motivated to orient themselves toward agreement on fair principles of cooperation. If Rawls did not presuppose this core normative disposition of respect and some ontological figure of dignity that orients it, then the notion of reasonable would have to contract to something weaker—and thus less useful—such as "exercising the basic capacities of reason and conversing in good faith."[17]

What exactly is the status in Rawls's theory of this implicit affirmation of dignity and equal respect? Larmore thinks Rawls is not as clear as he should be about this issue.[18] Rawls does not claim that his theory of justice is totally freestanding in relation to all moral-ontological foundations. He admits that it may require the affirmation of some minimal content; but such affirmation is justified only if it is "necessary to the political aim of consensus."[19] Presumably, Rawls would find this to be the case with regard to dignity and respect, although he does not explicitly say so. If he did clearly affirm dignity and equal respect, would that mean he owes us some sort of further justification of its foundational character? Probably not; rather he would argue that his affirmation merely reflects what is already a widely shared assumption in "modern democratic society." It is simply the cultural presence of this affirmation that is the key issue for getting his conception of justice started.[20] As long as dignity and respect are affirmed, he need not look further into issues of how such an affirmation is justified.

This stance is plausible from the point of view of Rawls's intention to construct a political conception of the justice of the "basic structure" of a society.[21] But from the broader perspective I am taking in this book—an ethos of late-modern citizenship—such a stance of nonengagement with the foundational issues above cannot be justified. The reason for this is that such an ethos inquires not only about the justness of basic structures but also about how we go about "living . . . the structures" (in Charles Taylor's words).[22] This means we must be as concerned with everyday dispositions and motivations as we are with fundamental structures. Rawls does, of course, imagine that citizens who live in a fully just state would adequately internalize his basic principles and thus spontaneously support such an order. But perhaps the matter of individual obligation and motivation in the midst of political contest would never be so simple. If so, then even in a relatively just polity one would need to think further about how a given ethos might, here and now, bias the reproduction of social structures in directions that are more rather than less hospitable to justice.[23]

A useful way of understanding what is at issue here might be to consider the range of concerns expressed by J. S. Mill in *On Liberty*. Mill certainly wants to have a political system with just constitutional and other legal structures. But he is also concerned with a broader ethos of citizenship that will help motivate individuals to go beyond the minimum obligation to obey just laws. This broader ethos emerges in relation to what is, in essence, a basic insight about social life in modern democratic societies; namely, the emergence of the threat of a "tyranny of . . . prevailing opinion and feeling."[24] This danger is presented by the pressure to conform to majority opinion that operates not just inside of the constitutional and legal structure but also outside of it. In this context, one can see Mill as appealing to an ethos that reaches beyond legal obligation. It draws its cognitive and motivational force from the moral foundation to which he appeals; that is, his basic sense of what a morally progressive individual and society look like.

For this sort of ethos to be robustly sustained in everyday life, one would expect the foundation animating judgment and action to be consistently scrutinized, refined, and drawn upon, as we confront new situations to which it must be applied. As long as we stay with Rawls's structural portrait, we are not expected to have to draw upon foundations in such situation-inflected ways. But at the level of ethos, where we are pressed by this expectation of congruence between a specific situation requiring judgment, on the one hand, and our foundational commitment, on the other, it seems plausible to think that we will begin to discover ways in which the implications of our foundations will run counter to those of others.

In sum, one can say that an ethos of late-modern citizenship might motivate us to affirm some *political* conception of justice (for example, Rawls's or a roughly comparable, procedural one, such as Habermas's) to a substantial degree, but it will not insulate us entirely from mutual engagement and contestation regarding how our ethical-ontological foundations draw us toward some courses of action versus others.[25] Given that such an ethos thus cannot avoid some entanglement with foundational issues, what guidance might it provide at this more basic level of reflection?

II. Site Two: Ontological Sources

An adequate answer to the foregoing question will require, first, some general account of the activity of reflecting on one's most basic beliefs and commitments. I will argue that the two most familiar ways of envisioning such reflection—uncovering foundations and choosing frameworks—are insufficiently sensitive to the challenges of late modernity. More adequate would be a variant of the account Charles Taylor offers with his notion of "sources of the self."[26] I want to elucidate this model, showing how and why it is superior for present purposes to the two more familiar ones (A). Then I turn to fleshing out the way such a portrait of our ethical-ontological background helps specify the sort of attentiveness and restraint that would have to be displayed at this site by a reasonable individual (B).

A. *Modes of Reflection on Sources*

In its most general sense, reflection upon what is basic to human beings is a search for meaning in light of human finitude. I mean by finitude, first, that we have foreknowledge of our mortality; and, second, that this knowledge tinges important aspects of our lives, whether we want it to or not.[27] When we think of reflecting upon what gives our lives meaning, we tend, as I suggested previously, to gravitate toward one of two models for comprehending such a search. We tend to envision ourselves, on the one hand, as uncovering, or *discovering*, a foundation that possesses authority because of its transcendent character; or, on the other hand, as *choosing* the most basic immanent framework of values that will then have priority over all our other values.[28] I will briefly delineate these two models and then suggest that each is too one-sided to fully capture the insights that press upon us as late-modern individuals. In this regard, we do better to affirm a model that captures some qualities of *both* discovery and choice.

In the foundations model, we envision ourselves digging down to discover what animates and lends certainty to our lives and the commitments that guide them. The figure of depth is intended to signal the existence of what is transcendent, or beyond the everyday, something permanent and infinite that awaits fuller illumination. The truth, or rightness, thus discovered gains its peculiar affective and cognitive force precisely because it resides beyond the everyday. The figure of God represents the most familiar such foundation.

Alternatively, we might see the activity of reflection on basics as a kind of periodic cognitive checkup of the relation between our judgments and beliefs in everyday life, on the one hand, and our considered support for them, on the other. This supporting structure, or framework, of belief is one we have chosen or freely affirmed; its greater authority for us rests in a crucial way on the condition that we have willed it. Things could have been otherwise; I could have willed completely differently, and I may in the future. Utilitarianism is an example of a philosophical perspective that would have us see authority in this fashion.[29] One simply has full sovereign authority over oneself and exercises it by making choices and arranging preferences related to one's values and principles.

Taylor construes the character of reflection on basic matters quite differently. Let me first contrast his alternative with the foundations model. In place of the excavation of foundations, he substitutes the "articulation" of "sources."[30] Although both imply a gesture of working toward the illumination of something crucial to one's practical investments, Taylor's picture embodies key differences. Part of this difference follows from everyday connotations. The achievement of clarifying foundations has a strong connotation of enhancing my knowledge, of *making my beliefs more solid* by illuminating the ground of their truth. Having recourse to "sources" can certainly have something of this sense. But it can also carry the implication of *being sustained or refreshed* by the clearer water one finds by journeying up a stream, even if its ultimate source always remains out of reach.

Taylor affirms the latter, ordinary meaning, and adds two other dimensions that give his account of attending to "sources of the self" its peculiar shape. The first of these is that the process of seeking one's sources involves not only discovering but also creating and choosing. Within the foundations model, exploration is typically construed as a clearing away of the earth that obscures a fuller view of one's sources. In short, something already there but not in sight is progressively brought to light. But the light metaphor is misleading. According to Taylor, the process of bringing a source into language is itself unavoidably creative; no meanings stand fully present to themselves outside of language, awaiting only a moment of photographic illumination. This characteristic is related to another, namely, that one never attains full articulacy in regard to sources. As the world throws up new experiences, I must progressively bring them to bear on the sources that animate me. There is no point of completion or full articulacy, both because my life is open ended and because articulacy is always achieved in the medium of ordinary language, in relation to which I can never find sovereign transparency.[31] Our mortality means, of course, that there will be an end to this interpretation; but cessation does not equate to fullness of articulation.

Such characteristics make the activity of articulation take on the qualities of a quest or a process of continually working on a puzzle.[32] One always seeks greater insight; but since full articulacy always remains up ahead, the dispositional qualities I manifest within the activity of searching itself become as important as the intimations I might have of the ultimate goal of my journey or of the character of the completed puzzle.

One further contrast between the two models must also be highlighted. Within the picture of excavating foundations, hard work is supposed to discover, or draw out, something of essentially fixed shape and solidity whose significance is then rendered fully evident. In effect, I know then where I stand and I know the ground is solid. This image of clarity, solidity, and epistemological certainty stands in sharp contrast to Taylor's, which has no fixed endpoint, no certainty about the truth of one's beliefs. In a world where it is a source that I articulate, I may justifiably come to feel the deepest and strongest commitment to that source, but I should never mistakenly equate that with increasing certainty of knowledge. In short, a deepening of commitment that sustains me more robustly does not equate to a growing cognitive certainty that my commitments deserve to promptly trump others that they encounter.

Thus the one-sidedness of the foundations model lies in its adherence to the notion that reflecting on basics is a matter of enhancing my conviction of truth. When I operate with this portrait, I have located the other who contests my views between the truth and me. This creates a persistent tendency to script the other as an obstacle to my further elaboration and implementation of the truth. The danger this might entail for ethical-political life is readily apparent.

At this point, a glance back at Rawls is helpful. He emphasizes a late-modern insight whose affirmation helps keep us from succumbing to the preceding, dangerous train of thought. A reasonable person, he tells us, will admit to the persistence of "burdens of judgment." This means that one will recognize that the attempt to insert comprehensive foundational truths into the basic arrangements of a polity is an exercise that is almost certain to go wrong.[33] The admission that there are such burdens, or challenges, affecting the reliability of one's judgments is clearly one of the primary lessons learned by modern Western societies from the Reformation to the present.

A proponent of the articulation model would certainly affirm Rawls's way of trying to operationalize this lesson in the form of recognizing the burdens of judgment; he would, however, also argue that a late-modern ethos applying to the site of basic matters requires more of us. For Rawls, we can clearly distinguish those "reasonable comprehensive doctrines" that have taken to heart the fact of pluralism from the unreasonable ones that have not.[34] For a late-modern ethos, however, things are not so clear-cut. Such an ethos certainly affirms the idea of a distinction like this one, but it also has to be more attentive to the fact that lessons are sometimes less-than-fully learned or susceptible to degrees of qualification that deplete their power to guide action. This worry is hardly hypothetical in the post-9/11 era, especially in the United States. President George W. Bush referred to the ensuing war on terror as a "crusade"; and he made it clear that God had affirmed the decision to invade Iraq.[35] Such statements, as well as the 2004 prisoner abuse scandal at Abu Ghraib and the recent pressure to curb civil liberties within the United States, should make us entertain seriously the possibility that a significant sector of the American population may increasingly envision the United States as something like a "Christian security state." If this heady mix of ideas gains ground, it will do so because that sector thinks that the stakes of the monumental struggle before us are so clear that the normal burdens of judgment are suspended.

In the context of such worries, one can see more clearly why imagining our most fundamental commitments in terms of the articulation model would appear to be more reasonable than imagining them in terms of the foundations model. The latter typically envisions human dignity as warranted by our status as agents of God's truth. The difficulty with this ontological figure, however, is that despite all the historical lessons learned, it still often draws truth and absoluteness together in ways that can drift in politically dangerous directions.

In what way might an affirmation of the articulation model render us potentially less susceptible to such a drift? The answer to this question rests on the elucidation of a different figuration of dignity that is as congruent with that model as the figure of the agent of God's truth is with the foundations model. The shape of this alternative figure will emerge in stages through the remainder of this chapter, as well as in the following two. For the moment, let me just say that the figure is that of a continual *traveler* with a distinctive sort of disposition and consciousness. At this point, the only crucial thing to understand about such a figure of dignity is that its character would be such as to make it unreasonable for this being to imagine itself in possession of the fullness of truth about its sources and thus encouraged to divide its world into those fateful and self-righteous categories of believers of truth, on the one hand, and their opponents, on the other. The implication of this insight is that the expectation of reasonableness has to find some foothold already at the site of sources and not just when we arrive at the site of fair terms of cooperation, as within Rawls's project.

The articulation model makes it possible to imagine the soft collar of reasonableness being brought to bear at the site of basic matters, because it puts the linguistically mediated character of human being at the center of the process of articulation. Sources cannot be directly revealed in any fashion not mediated by language and thus involving all the difficulties inherent to any process of interpretation. Taylor takes this to be another central, late-modern insight, one that emerged with the linguistic turn in philosophy, especially in Wittgenstein, Heidegger, and Gadamer in the mid-twentieth century. When we consider reflection upon basic matters in light of this insight, it helps us to comprehend the shortcomings of the foundations model and the kind of subtle gravitational force certainty of belief exerts on it.

This issue opens onto a related sense in which the articulation model honors what I called earlier "the anxiety of finitude" rather than seeking to repress or transcend it. The problem with the foundations model in this regard is that it posits human being's mortality in such a way that the gravitational force toward what is solid, transcendent, and infinite feeds a perfectly understandable wish not to ponder attentively the character of finitude. That condition becomes merely a temporary, inessential one, away from which my attention ought to be directed.[36]

It might be objected at this point that the foregoing criticisms of the foundations model all tend in the same direction; namely, toward disqualifying from the start any variant of theism. But that is not the case. Here it is useful to remember that Taylor develops his articulation model in the context of a broad case for a kind of theism that is responsive to the central challenges of late modernity. His is a theism able to engage quietly and persistently with finitude, especially as it is manifest in our character as linguistically mediated beings. What is most important to emphasize at this point is simply that the embrace of the articulation model does not stack the deck against theism.[37]

It might be helpful to illustrate this with a historical example that shows how a theist can effectively function within the frame of the articulation model, even if the individual understands himself to be operating with the foundations model. Consider the remarkable mid-eighteenth-century American Quaker, John Woolman. In one sense, he might seem to be a powerful example of an advocate of the pure model of discovering sources. His commitment to leading an exemplary Christian life is unquestionable, as is his sense that his beliefs stood on an "immutable foundation."[38] But what makes Woolman so fascinating in the present context is the way he was able to express his *deepest commitment* to religion without allowing his conduct to manifest the self-righteousness and moral rigorism toward others that is so often the effect of *absolute conviction*.[39]

Woolman did not consider himself a theologian, nor was he politically active in any normal sense. Although his home was a farm outside of Philadelphia, he spent much of his adult life traveling extensively to colonies south of Pennsylvania where slavery had its deepest roots. There he would methodically visit, and often stay, in the homes of slave owners. During his visits, he would quietly but persistently raise the issue of slavery. Woolman did not conceive his work to be that of preaching the truth, but rather that of expressing his commitment to Christian teachings that he felt required him to continually bear witness to the issue of slavery in the presence of his hosts. He never presumed to know what God required others to do; he knew only that he had to express his opposition to slavery and concern for the souls of those who kept slaves.

In the early 1760s, during an outbreak of violence between the settlers in western Pennsylvania and the Delaware tribe, Woolman, against all advice, traveled to one of the Indian villages "to spend some time with [them] that I might feel and understand their life and the spirit they live in, [to see] if haply I might receive some instruction from them, or if they be in any degree helped forward by my following the leadings of Truth amongst them."[40] In this instance, as in so many others in his life, Woolman seems to have been an individual who knew that he was always "on the way" to a deeper understanding of his sources, never in their full presence.

I want to turn now from what has been shown to be the one-sidedness of the foundations model to the claim that the chosen-framework model is comparably guilty. Its problem of one-sidedness, however, is just the opposite of the sort foundationalism displays; that is, the problem now is an overemphasis on creating and choosing as opposed to an overemphasis on the discovery of that which has essential solidity, authority, and truth prior to the activity of trying to comprehend it.

The chosen-framework model is oriented to gaining clarity in the name of getting greater potential control over all aspects of our lives. The increase in control promises, in turn, to increase freedom and happiness. The idea of fulfilling this promise is one of our core Enlightenment legacies. The problem in the present context is expressed in the following question: What effect is there when we figure reflection upon the most basic matters of our lives along these lines? One might describe this change as one of willing all that is the background of our lives into the foreground where it can be more manageably entered into rational calculations about our happiness. But when we have committed ourselves to such a task, we have also thereby implicitly embraced an ontological figure of humans as sovereign entities. As Burke, Adorno, and Foucault all realized in different ways, once this occurs, we have fashioned ourselves as figures whose wills are in principle unlimited and whose reason is in no need of chastening. Here there emerges that will to infinitude about which such critics of modernity wish to warn us. It is crucial in thinking about this danger not to limit our concern to the most visible and grandly egregious variants, such as Burke observed in the French Revolution, or recent generations have observed in twentieth-century fascism and state socialism. We need to worry as well about the less-obtrusive variants such as Foucault highlights with his notion of disciplines that seem to spread almost without specific human intention.

B. Sources and Reasonableness

So far I have attempted to sketch out a picture of the general terrain upon which we can reflect on basic matters in a fashion that is sensitive to the challenges and insights of late modernity. Now I turn to the question of what it would mean to conform to the call to be reasonable as we articulate our sources in relation to one another. More specifically, how do we construe the attentiveness and restraint that largely constitute the fulfillment of the expectation of reasonableness?

Attentiveness would be displayed by an affirmation of the twofold character of the articulation of sources: the sense in which such reflection involves both discovery and creation. In being so attentive, I continually remind myself of the ways in which some accounts of basic matters require us to repress too many of the insights that we late-modern citizens have. The criterion of restraint is displayed in the acceptance of the insight that in pursuing basic matters we are always left with something less than full articulacy; and thus the next "other" I meet may hold something crucial to a fuller understanding of my sources. When restraint is comprehended in this way as oriented around the articulation model, it is not difficult to see how virtues of carefulness and humility toward the other are prefigured more clearly here than is the case in either the foundations model or the framework model, where the other is more susceptible to being quickly scripted as either an obstacle or an entity of possible instrumental use.

Attentiveness and restraint gain their content in relation to that figure of a journey that I have suggested is implied in the notion of articulating sources. Reasonableness accordingly refers us to the orientation of a traveler who has a rough sense of the direction in which she must head but is also crucially dependent on the insights of those she meets along the way for clues as to her ultimate destination. Additionally, she knows that although she may gain an increasingly fuller sense of that destination, she will nevertheless remain a traveler who is always still on her way to that destination. One might even call this traveling figure a *pilgrim*, when she travels beyond the boundaries of her comfort zone, geographically and culturally.[41] According to the *OED*, the term does not necessarily involve a religious dimension, although it is certainly open to including either that or possibly the unorthodox moral-spiritual dimension of an ethos that prizes virtues such as modesty, humility, attentiveness, and self-restraint in its initial encounters on foreign landscapes (both literal and figurative).

The construal of dignity around the portrait of the anxious but quietly committed traveler is certainly not uncontroversial in its figuration of human being or in its affinity for some ethical virtues rather than others. But then no portrait can guarantee that it will meet with universal agreement. The real issue is not whether it is uncontroversial, but whether it coheres with central, late-modern insights, and whether it might be more inclusive than, say, the traditional, theistically based figurations. And, on this point, the figure of the perpetual traveler whose encounter with life quietly and persistently honors its subjection to mortality seems better able to include at least some theists as well as some nontheists.[42]

I want to turn now to the third aspect of my late-modern account of reasonableness. Just as I showed earlier that reasonableness in relation to fair terms of cooperation implies an engagement with reasonableness in relation to the articulation of sources, I now want to suggest that reasonableness in the latter sense is also similarly entangled with reasonableness in relation to the demand for the recognition of identity. What is the nature of this entanglement, and what exactly does reasonableness amount to on this third site?

III. Site Three: The Recognition of Identity

If we think of agents and their articulation of sources, it seems to follow pretty clearly that what agents take to be their identity is constitutively involved with that process. The horizon provided by that articulation allows me to know where I stand in moral space; as Taylor nicely puts it: "To know who I am is a species of knowing where I stand."[43] Now part of what is involved in this interconnection is my identity in a universalizable sense. As we saw in Sections I and II, one thing that an ethos of reasonableness expects of us is a recognition of your and my status as persons who possess dignity and who are thus deserving of respect. Obviously such recognition is significant, but just as obviously this dimension does not incorporate all of what, over the last few decades, has been referred to with the phrases "identity politics" and "the politics of recognition."[44] These phrases draw our attention beyond respect for persons in the universalistic sense, to the acknowledgment of people's diversity, their distinctiveness of language, religion, sexuality, nationality, and traditional practices. This demand that one's identity be acknowledged in its distinctiveness, or difference, is one of the most controversial subjects in contemporary political theory. So it is important to emphasize that my analysis of this site of reflection has a limited aim. I am only trying to elucidate a certain spirit, or disposition, that can be brought to the reflection on, and contestation of, such issues under the banner of a certain sort of claim to reason. Such a spirit, or disposition, will constitute part of a reasonable, fivefold, late-modern ethos.

As a way of initially engaging this topic, let me return to the beginning of this chapter, where I discussed some twentieth-century critics of the Enlightenment's understanding of reason. For such critics, Enlightenment reason carries an unacknowledged will to dominate inside of its more admirable manifestations. Thus the will to know, to construct, to control, to resolve, and to reconcile are all more ambivalent in their effects than was originally thought in the eighteenth century, when the "party of reason" arrayed itself categorically against the party of ignorance, superstition, and domination. One key site where reason and domination evolve as coconspirators rather than as simple opponents is in the construction and reproduction of the identity of the self. The process of constructing myself as an epitome of enlightenment—that is, as a free, rational, and responsible being—can only proceed by means of contrasts. In other words, the construction of my identity necessarily involves the simultaneous construction of others, even if only implicitly, who are unfree, irrational, and irresponsible—in short, nonsovereign and potentially threatening. Prominent examples of this dynamic at work in the history of the United States include the way Native Americans were positioned in relation to the expansion westward of white civilization, especially in the nineteenth century, and the way the identity of the "Un-American" was engendered in the mid-twentieth century during the Cold War. In the last couple decades, the exposure of this dark side of Enlightenment reason has sometimes seemed so thoroughgoing as to vitiate entirely any ideal of constructing an admirable, late-modern self within the traditions of modern, enlightened reason. But that conclusion betrays a perfectly resistible desire to oversimplify what is in fact a complicated issue.[45]

I intend rather to unpack some of the philosophical complexity that resides upon this problematic site, and then see if some other conclusion might be warranted; more specifically, one that allows us to see how a sense of reasonableness might infuse the discourse of identity recognition. Toward this end, it is useful to begin by separating two insights about identity and difference that are at the core of the critique of our Enlightenment legacy. The first informs us that identity and difference stand in a mutually constitutive relationship at the ontological level. A process of identity formation is always simultaneously a process of difference formation. And this means that identity will always be ontologically indebted to difference. The second insight builds upon the first and shows how modern ideas of the self as free, rational, and responsible have given rise to particular historical formations of difference within whose scope all manner of groups had the misfortune to fall.

The combined weight of these two insights would seem to constitute a solid battering ram against any comforting talk about enlightenment, because it seems necessarily to implicate reason as a central coconspirator in perpetuating some of the great injustices that have accompanied Western colonization and enlightenment. We can, however, resist such an implication if we focus attention on exactly how we understand the relationship between these two insights. Consider the way in which I initially introduced them. They appear to be constitutively joined. For example, the identity of nineteenth-century white Americans as the active subjects of the geographic extension of reason and freedom necessarily and simultaneously constituted Native Americans in such a way as to insure that their distinctiveness would be denied recognition. And, of course, that would make it more justifiable (and thus easier on the conscience) to treat them in barbaric ways. The upshot of grasping the relation of the two insights in this fashion has rather stark consequences for how we understand identity and recognition. By this I mean that once the relationship is understood in this way, then the very process of identity formation itself is always already implicated in the *mis*recognition of the other.

Accordingly, if I ask what I can do to alleviate the harms arising from such misrecognition, an adequate answer will require me to go back to the most basic level of my identity constitution; more specifically, I must somehow deconstruct my identity from the ground up. That is the only way to relieve the pressure of misrecognition. Perhaps the most prominent example of this logic of identity is contained in Judith Butler's *Gender Trouble*.[46] There she seems to be saying that the only way to interrupt the fateful relation between identity formation and misrecognition is to engage in a process of continual, "insistent rifting" of my identity.[47] In short, to extend recognition to the

other, I must renounce the idea of an identity that has coherence and continuity. As critics pointed out, this makes it seem as though the very idea of a
stable identity is "inherently oppressive."[48]

Clearly, such an extreme remedy for the ills of misrecognition could not
qualify as something one should feel compelled to administer to oneself as a
result only of the soft pull of reasonableness. It may be that one cannot even
coherently imagine what it would mean to be like the mythic Penelope "per-
petually undoing the identities one is nevertheless bound to construct."[49] Is
there, however, an alternative way of conceiving the problem of identity and
recognition within which we can identify a remedy, the recourse to which
might qualify as reasonable?

In fact, a place exists on this problematic terrain at which an appeal to the
reasonable might plausibly be seen as getting a foothold. This place becomes
increasingly evident the more we think in terms of teasing apart the two
insights about identity, recognition, and misrecognition. The most cogent effort in this regard comes from William Connolly.[50] He fully accepts the insight about identity and difference being constitutively implicated ontologically
with one another. But he differentiates between the construction of difference intrinsically entailed by the constitution of my identity, on the one
hand, and an at least partially separable, resilient "temptation that readily in-
sinuates itself" into that onto-logic, on the other.

> An identity is established in relation to a series of differences that have
> become socially recognized. These differences are essential to its being.
> If they did not coexist as differences, it would not exist in its distinctness
> and solidity. Entrenched in this indispensable relation is a second set of
> tendencies, themselves in need of exploration, to congeal established
> identities into fixed forms, thought and lived as if their structure ex-
> pressed the true order of things. When these pressures prevail, the main-
> tenance of one identity (or field of identities) involves the conversion of
> some differences into otherness, into evil, or one of its numerous surro-
> gates. Identity requires difference in order to be, and it converts differ-
> ence into otherness in order to secure its own self-certainty.[51]

This temptation toward self-certainty varies historically and can be resisted by
various means. A distinctive emphasis in modern Western culture has been

control, or mastery, of the world around us. This persistent orientation—as well as the underlying anxiety of finitude that persistently activates it—makes us especially vulnerable to the temptation that Connolly identifies.[52] In short, whatever cannot be mastered or comprehended within familiar categories draws upon itself the status of something that, or of someone who, is a potential threat to the security and sovereignty of my identity.

In relation to *this* propensity, we can reasonably be expected to show some self-restraint. Such a disposition does not require a wholesale deconstructing of my own identity. But it does require more work on the self than the sort of commitment to tolerance that received its classical expression in Mill's work. In saying this, I don't mean to denigrate Mill. He certainly realized that intolerance is deeply ingrained in human life; and, as I suggested earlier, he tried to combat this by looking not just to legal structures, but also to an ethos that might suffuse all of public life and slacken the insistent pressure of majority opinion.[53] Nevertheless, Mill does not give us an adequate understanding of the roots of intolerance and other associated modes of denigrating those who are constituted as the others of our late-modern projects and identities. One value of putting things in these terms is that it provides us with a plausible way of comprehending how Mill can be so eloquent about liberty and simultaneously make his infamous remarks about non-Western peoples as "barbarians" who must be constrained by colonial powers to accept the forms of Western civilization.[54]

To draw ourselves away from similar mistakes, we need to locate the roots of this whole complex of issues concerning otherness in the temptations associated with the highly charged process of identity consolidation. Only after this shift of attention will we be capable of sketching out what a reasonable late-modern ethos might ask of us on this site. The processes of pluralization and globalization today exert enormous pressure on the self as it tries to adhere to the elusive ideal of the sovereign, rational, and responsible human being. These pressures can evoke a continual low-grade fear of, or hostility to, diversity, as well as frustration with a political world that so often seems to disappoint those excessive, normalizing expectations about what the world owes us.[55] A late-modern ethos would ask us to develop strategies of the self that work toward dampening that hostility and moderating those expectations. Strategies of this sort have been elaborated by a number of contemporary philosophers who are wrestling with questions of late-modern life.

These efforts might usefully be comprehended as different ways of portraying the idea of an ethos of "presumptive generosity" toward the other. Examples would include "critical responsiveness" (Connolly); "fundamentally more capacious, generous and 'unthreatened' bearings of the self" (Butler, in work after *Gender Trouble*); "hospitality" (Derrida); "receptive generosity" (Romand Coles); and "opening ourselves to the surprises" of engagement with the other (Patchen Markell).[56] Crucial in all of these perspectives is a sense of the cognitive and affective need to dampen the initial wariness and certainty that we are likely to carry into our engagement with those whom we all too easily size up as radically other to us.[57]

Gathering together the threads of the preceding discussion, I can now specify more directly what it would mean to respond to the call to be reasonable in the recognition of identity. The sense of attentiveness is to be attached to a willingness to continually be receptive to the distinction between the onto-logic of the mutual constitution of identity and difference, on the one hand, and the psychosocial temptation to transform difference into otherness, on the other hand.[58] And the sense of restraint to which the expectation of reasonableness would bind us is shown in the willingness to resist this temptation. One of the primary means of doing this effectively lies in the cultivation of an initial generosity—a willful, temporary suspension of the engagement of my full, critical apparatus of practical judgment.

When we construe the call to reasonableness in this way, we are subtly repositioning it as a virtue appropriate to the self as *host*, as the one who stands on familiar ground and crafts the affective and cognitive terms upon which he will respond to the approach of another to his door. The figure of the host is as central here to an enlarged sense of reasonableness as is the figure of the traveler in the space of articulating sources.

As we imagine this central role of the host in identity recognition, it is also crucial to acknowledge that it cannot be construed in isolation from the first site of reason-giving; namely, where the underlying fairness of the terms of interaction is at issue. By itself, the ethos of the admirable host forms a sphere of reasonable engagement; but when it is so construed, it may mask structures of power and privilege that can, in turn, inconspicuously corrupt the scene of hospitality. To say this is merely to emphasize that the dynamic of identity recognition always operates against a background of social relations and structures that embodies claims about justice and injustice. In short, the third sphere of reasonableness must also always be understood as constitutively entangled with the first.

IV. Conclusion

The idea that practical reason in its emphatic sense should guide political life has come in for some hard knocks over the last century or so. One cannot ignore these blows. But neither is one obliged to abandon the idea of emphatic reason as thoroughly trounced. Accordingly, in this chapter I have begun the task of delineating a minimal, or chastened, account of the expectations of reasonableness as they can be construed today across three spaces, or sites, where we are challenged to give reasons for our conduct. With this threefold account, I have started to fill in the substance of a late-modern ethos of citizenship. Chapters 4 and 5 will add the two remaining folds. But first it is necessary for me to flesh out more clearly the specific character of the self or subject that I imagine being capable of sustaining such an ethos.

3

After Critique: Affirming Subjectivity

In Chapter 2, I began to delineate how the ethos I am proposing can understand itself as a reasonable response to a set of late-modern challenges. In the
process of elucidating this claim, I also implicitly began to sketch the outlines
of a figure of the self, or subject, who might sustain the sort of expectations
that this reasonableness would demand. In this chapter, I want to attend
more closely to the various qualities such a figure must have. But before undertaking this specific constructive task, I need to explain the general philosophical context in which it is being taken up. I am interested particularly in
the way in which the mainstream, modern conception of the self has come to
be seen by many as the persistent, if not intentional, perpetrator of the harms
attributed to the modern Western conception of reason. This familiar subject
of reason, freedom, and dignity has been the object of sustained critique in
the last few decades at the hands of, notably, poststructuralists, postmodernists, feminists, communitarians, and critical theorists. The charge against
this figure is that it has presented itself as the flower of Western civilization,
without admitting that it has simultaneously been the carrier of resilient patterns of domination and self-delusion that critics have tended to associate
with modern reason, as we saw in Chapter 2. How legitimate is this indict-
ment of the modern subject? And, if it is legitimate, at least to some degree,
how do we proceed in its aftermath; that is, what kind of figuration of subjectivity might not fall victim to such potent critiques?

Let me start with a very rough characterization of the modern moral-
political subject as it stands at the bar of late-modern judgment: *He* is conceived as *disengaged* from his social background and oriented toward *mastery* of
the world that confronts him; nevertheless, he can *discover*, by the light of *reason*,
universally applicable principles of justice, grounded in some *foundationalist*

account of God, nature, progress, or human communication that can become the basis of a constructive political *consensus* with other individuals. This complex of characteristics (or, more typically, some subset) has been the target of a variety of twentieth-century thinkers from Heidegger to feminism, from Carl Schmitt to Foucault and postmodernism, from Horkheimer and Adorno to Charles Taylor.

If one asks about the kind of political theory within which this notion of subjectivity most clearly emerged and thrived, the familiar answer is liberalism. Today one typically hears the term *liberal subject* used pretty much as a synonym for *modern subject.* Any attempt either to assess the legitimacy of the critique of modern subjectivity or to try to think in its aftermath is thus necessarily involved with evaluating some aspects of the liberal tradition.

Contemporary liberals often take strong exception to the attempt to identify their tradition with the foregoing portrait of modern subjectivity. Thus, for example, they sometimes claim that the liberal subject is not necessarily gendered male; or that although some liberals, such as Locke, affirm a subject oriented toward mastery of nature, others, such as J. S. Mill, do not.

Against this background of contested claims, I want to suggest that one can identify some features of the modern subject that are indeed characteristics of the liberal subject. Further, I want to consider why these particular features have been legitimately subjected to critique, and what progress can be made toward thinking subjectivity in the aftermath of that critique. This thinking in the aftermath will have to recognize in very specific ways, however, that it cannot simply divorce itself from liberalism. A figure of subjectivity that is developed enough to sustain the sort of late-modern ethos I envision will have to be one that both accommodates the legitimate insights of the critique and does justice to the liberal tradition.

My goal can be stated in a preliminary way as follows: Critics of liberalism often accuse liberal subjectivity of an overemphasis on the disengaged individual whose capaciousness includes the ability to reason his way through political strife by means of consensual frameworks whose effect is to tame the worst sources of conflict. In opposition to this portrait, critics argue that we must understand that political life is deeply agonistic and thus not so amenable to the reason and consensus of the liberal individual. Ultimately, I am going to align myself with this agonistic counterportrait, at least to a degree. But it is important to stress that the ethical and ontological basis of agonism can be conceived in more than one fashion; and these bases can be more or less successful in their critiques of liberal subjectivity. I will start by examining a currently popular line of attack that is rooted in the ideas of the early twentieth-century German jurist and political theorist Carl Schmitt. He is perhaps the most prominent source today for what one might call an *unrelenting* agonism. Against this, I will defend a *tempered* agonism.

My strategy for negotiating a path through this thicket of ideas will be to start by elaborating how agonism understands its critique of liberal subjectivity. As I just noted, I will distinguish two versions of agonism and suggest that the second—tempered agonism—is more persuasive (Section I). After that, I will examine how contemporary liberalism fights back. The most effective counterattack comes from *political* liberalism (Section II). Finally, I show how the agonistic critique can assume a *tempered* form that is both defensible in relation to liberalism and a worthy bearer of the particular sort of late-modern ethos I affirm (Section III).

I. The Modern Subject and Its Problems

To keep my undertaking down to a manageable size, I have to focus on some aspects of the critique and leave others aside. A moment ago, I presented a condensed sketch of the modern subject as indicted by its critics. In this section, I will focus only on the following portions of the portrait: first, the idea of disengaged selves who, through the use of reason, discover universal consensual principles of justice; and, second, the idea that what animates these selves is the foundational certainty that their orientation is warranted by God, nature, progress, reason, or the necessary implications of communication.

For the purposes of this section, I will assume that such an account of subjectivity has been present in liberalism. In what follows, I cannot hope to do full justice to the immense variety of attacks that have been launched against this account. But because I am concerned not just with the legitimacy of the attacks but also with what we can say about moral and political subjectivity in their aftermath, it is reasonable to start by giving disproportionate attention to one particular issue: the unsettling asymmetry between the systematically developed character of many of the critiques of subjectivity, on the one hand, and the subsequent, rather vague quality of affirmative thinking in the aftermath, on the other.

Using this issue as a guiding concern, a productive way of proceeding is to consider the recent revival of interest in Carl Schmitt. Some contemporary critics have discovered a strong resonance between their own insights and Schmitt's assaults on liberal ideas of subjectivity, reason, and politics. But the discovery of this resonance with Schmitt is accompanied by a quite prickly challenge. Unlike some of the twentieth century's other radical critics of subjectivity, such as Heidegger or Horkheimer and Adorno, Schmitt articulates a very explicit portrait of what a postliberal politics should look like. The difficulty is that it is a deeply fascist one.[1] Thus, the challenge Schmitt clearly presents for today's critics is to elucidate more carefully how the affirmative normative impulses in their perspectives can *both* maintain the desired opposition to liberal subjectivity *and* simultaneously establish enough distance from the deeply authoritarian notion of subjectivity and politics associated with Schmitt's unrelenting agonism.[2]

To draw out what is at issue in this bind, I will look briefly at Schmitt, as well as at how Chantal Mouffe has recently attempted to use his ideas for the critique of subjectivity and yet avoid becoming contaminated when she tries to think affirmatively in the aftermath (A). This investigation will unearth some substantial drawbacks to her attempt, particularly in regard to how it imagines the central idea of agonism and its relation to a possible ethos of late-modern subjectivity. Against the background of this flawed effort to think in the aftermath, it will be easier to see what kind of perspective might bear more promise. Here I will pick up and develop my discussion of identity and difference in the preceding chapter. The goal will be to develop a persuasive account of how one best negotiates the turn to an affirmative counter-portrait from within the tradition of critique (B). This account will be, in the terminology introduced previously, a tempered agonism; that is, one that draws upon a richer set of ontological figures than at least some proponents of unrelenting agonism.

After sketching what I take to be a persuasive representation of the critical tradition, I then turn to consider, in Section II, the liberal counter-charge that this entire critical tradition is deeply confused and, finally, possesses very little value for contemporary thought. When that counter-charge has been fully engaged, the plausibility of the sort of claims I want to make about subjectivity in the aftermath can begin to take clearer shape in Section III.

A. The Attractions of Carl Schmitt

Like today's critics, Schmitt finds fault with liberalism's ontological figure of a disengaged subject who reasons methodically toward an ever-more inclusive and consensual political order based on universal principles of justice. He posits instead a subject embedded in the affective solidarity of a kind of enlarged, *volkisch* friendship. And because friendship for him only comes to life against the contrasting category of foe or enemy, it means that this embeddedness is inherently connected with conflict. Politics for him is the ontologic of friends and enemies. This antagonism of "one fighting collectivity of people" versus another may subside temporarily, but it is ultimately unrelenting. The liberal onto-logic of rational, disengaged subjectivity glosses over this defining antagonism of political life. The liberal subject faces, from within its stance of disengagement, only either competitors who find that their attempts to master nature can be coordinated in a mutually beneficial way through markets, or other disengaged bearers of universal rights who are willing to reach a reciprocally beneficial consensus.[3]

Schmitt's ontological counterfigure of subjectivity and politics thus replaces disengagement with an embeddedness in a relationship to a people; and it replaces the potential for ever-more inclusive, consensually based political orders with the imperatives of conflict and exclusion. The work of the Schmittian subject is, first and foremost, that of struggling against the enemy who threatens its collective identity.

Although, as I have said, many of Schmitt's claims against liberalism resonate sympathetically with recent critics, the latter nevertheless want to part company with him when it comes to the unrelenting intensity of conflict between friend and enemy that opens out onto a fascist vista. The efforts of Chantal Mouffe to negotiate just such a partial divorce are highly instructive at this point. A brief examination of this effort will allow me to gain a more exact focus on the kind of novel normative shape that needs to be given to subjectivity in the aftermath.

Mouffe applauds Schmitt for seeing what the liberal tradition does not; namely, "the necessity of conflict as *the* crucial category of politics" (my emphasis). Politics just is about the "moment of closure" when some groups are excluded from a given political order. But Mouffe also wants to move this political ontology in a democratic direction. Accordingly, what is at issue most centrally for her is the struggle of the demos against elites for hegemony in a political order. The problem, of course, is how one is to imagine this struggle in a way that is not continually at risk of sliding back into Schmitt's deadly antagonism of friend and enemy. To prevent this, Mouffe appeals to a "liberal logic" to balance what would otherwise become an essentially Schmittian logic of coercive democratic hegemony.[4] Thus the dangerous side of the Schmittian conception of the political is to be continually blunted by recourse to essentially liberal notions such as the idea that political opponents must be dealt with in a restrained fashion, because they raise "legitimate" claims, and the idea that the open contest of such claims is a valid part of a pluralist polity.[5]

Once the Schmittian onto-logic receives this supplement, we have the means "to transform antagonism into agonism." What Mouffe wants to accomplish here is clear. Whether this joining of the Schmittian onto-logic of politics to the pluralist ethos of a restrained contest between legitimate adversaries is actually felicitous seems rather doubtful. Grounds for skepticism quickly become evident if one focuses on what it would mean to be the subject or bearer of such an orientation. It is difficult not to end up finding this subject to be cognitively and affectively implausible. She is oriented first and foremost to unrestrained conflict and the exclusion of the other based on collective identity; and yet she must also then affirm wholeheartedly the rights of the other and the fundamental legitimacy of political adversaries. Mouffe is quite clear about how radically this portrait of "a 'tamed' relation of antagonism" departs from Schmitt's political ontology.[6] But she seems entirely unconcerned with how implausible and incongruous her portrait becomes in the absence of additional ontological figures and sources that could prefigure the kind of distinctly non-Schmittian ideals she expects her subject to affirm. Mouffe merely asserts that her subject will embody both a Schmittian ontology and a liberal ethos. But why will this ethos get any uptake whatsoever in the cognition and feelings of a Schmittian subject? Consider feelings. Mouffe goes out of her way to validate the role of the passions in her subjects as something crucial to the mobilization of individuals to struggle for, and identify with, the hegemony of the demos.[7] From whence, however, would an individual get the affective resources that might sustain attachments to ideals such as legitimate opposition or pluralism, as opposed to the sublimity of deadly conflict?

As Mouffe has sketched things, it is difficult to imagine her subject as having anything other than a strategic and "polemical" (her term), rather than an ethical, attachment to such ideals.[8] Accordingly, one might imagine a Mouffean subject affirming these ideals when in a defensive posture vis-à-vis a stronger antagonist, where they could be advantageous in helping to protect and enhance the former's interests. But when the strategic circumstances shift, and these ideals possibly become obstacles to these interests, I see no basis for imagining these subjects doing anything other than discarding liberal, pluralist niceties. And, if this is so, Mouffe's account of subjectivity is simply not differentiated enough in the right ways for one to expect that individuals would exercise the restraint necessary to an agonistic, as opposed to an antagonistic, political life.

I want to take Mouffe's bind to be one of broad significance for thinking in the aftermath of the critique of subjectivity. Let me frame the issue as follows: Is there a way of construing agonism and subjectivity so as to avoid a Schmittian fate? What is needed, in short, is a perspective within which one can better imagine an agonism sustained, but also restrained, by some sort of ethos; in short, a tempered agonism.

B. Toward a Tempered Agonism

Let us return to the discussion of Connolly's work on identity and difference in Chapter 2. He stands clearly in the tradition of critics of subjectivity and proponents of agonism.[9] His distinctiveness, as I began to show earlier, resides in the particular weak ontology he elaborates, and in how effectively he draws out of it an agonism that is tempered with an ethos of political generosity.[10]

The value of Connolly's work will appear more vividly if I start by probing a bit further into what seems to go awry in Mouffe's thinking about agonism. Her difficulties begin with the decision to fully embrace Schmitt's political ontology. Politics is, in its essence, the conflict of friend and foe, he contends, in the same way that aesthetics is, in its essence, about the beautiful and the ugly. Whenever there are human collectivities, we "cannot escape the logic of the political."[11]

For Schmitt, this central ontological figure of identity-as-conflict *determines our destiny* in politics: to have a collective identity just is to fight that which is different. From my point of view, Schmitt at times almost appears to affirm a strong ontology, even though he does not seem particularly interested in providing any elaborate foundationalist argument. At other times, he suggests that identity-as-conflict has "a concrete and existential sense"; but it is difficult to see what Schmitt means by this.[12] His account certainly cannot be a weak-ontological one in my sense, whereby an ontological figure can only *prefigure* our stance toward political phenomena; that is, cognitively, morally, aesthetically, and affectively dispose us in a certain way, rather than freezing in our destiny.

Interestingly, Mouffe has recently felt the need to be more persuasive in establishing the philosophical cogency of her attempt to both accept Schmitt and yet also "part company" with him on his most fundamental commitment. She now wants to bolster her position by deploying what is essentially the same argument about identity and difference as Connolly's, the development of which I discussed in the preceding chapter. In short, she seeks to clearly distinguish the ontological claim regarding the mutually constitutive character of identity and difference, on the one hand, from the claim regarding the tendency in any given identity to construe difference in a way that continually enhances hostility and conflict, on the other.[13]

But once Mouffe has taken this tack, I would claim that she must also divest her position of any residual Schmittian elements. There simply remains no ground for her continuing to assert that unlimited conflict is the primary governing concept in politics; or, to put it slightly differently, that "the ineradicability of antagonism" is our fate. In effect, Mouffe cannot plausibly carry through her particular strategy of thinking "both *with* and *against* Schmitt."[14]

At this point, a proponent of unrelenting agonism—one unadulterated by anything like an ethos of presumptive generosity—might reply that I have shown only that it is not wise to place all one's bets on Schmitt. Other sources are available for this sort of agonism. Nietzsche's name would likely surface here. His early essay "Homer on Competition" might seem to provide just what is needed.[15]

I will suggest that the essay is indeed a rich source for agonistic thought, but what is affirmed is more of a tempered, rather than an unrelenting, agonism. This piece is a short meditation on Hesiod's view that Eris, the Greek goddess of strife, is actually "two goddesses who have quite separate dispositions." One promotes war and deadly feuds; the other goads men to "competition" and "envy." Nietzsche sees the former holding sway in the " 'pre-Homeric' abyss of a gruesome savagery of hatred and pleasure in destruction," whereas the latter sustains the later "Hellenic idea of competition."[16] The genius and humanity of fifth-century Greece was its ability to hold the first Eris at bay by fostering a robust expression of the passions and ambitions of the second. In sum, the Greeks were thus able to distinguish clearly between agonism and antagonism. Nietzsche also makes it clear that the problem of agonism degenerating into antagonism was always a pressing one for the Greeks. He interprets the institution of ostracism as originally intended to reinvigorate competition whenever some prominent political leader seemed on the threshold of becoming too powerful.[17] But just as important as such external constraints on behavior were the internal ones; more specifically, the dispositions associated with the ideals of a Greek gentleman. As an illustration, Nietzsche relates the story of Miltiades the Younger, one of the heroes at the battle of Marathon. Despite his military fame and good fortune, he nevertheless could not get over the ill will he felt toward another citizen as a result of a quarrel earlier in his life. Consequently, he allowed his sense of self-control and generosity, or magnanimity, to be overcome by "a base lust for vengeance." He sunk back thereby into the "'pre Homeric'" abyss.

Thus it appears that a Nietzschean agonism is one that must be tempered at least partially by means of restraints internal to one's character. Generosity appears to be a crucial disposition in this regard. My intent is not to claim that the generosity, or magnanimity, Nietzsche associates with the aristocratic Greek man is identical to the presumptive generosity that I am affirming as crucial to a late-modern ethos, but rather only to indicate that Nietzsche's agonism does not reduce its understanding of strife and competition to a one-dimensional logic, such as Schmitt's friend versus enemy. Nor does Nietzsche try to provide us with an incongruous picture of the agonistic agent, as does Mouffe, when she yokes the idea of the different-as-enemy to the ideas of liberal pluralism. In Nietzsche, the ideal of agonism coheres with a character ideal of Greek nobility that, in turn, embodies a commitment to being generous.

At this point, we are ready to turn back to Connolly's understanding of identity and difference. We can now appreciate more fully the way in which it expresses the idea of agonism. Identity is indeed constituted by difference, but this ontological ground does not in itself specify unlimited conflict as our political destiny. The kinds and degrees of conflict in a given society are dependent on how pliant or resistant citizens are to a whole set of "temptations" or "pressures" to fundamentalize the play of identity and difference;

more specifically, pressures to fix some modes of difference as social categories of "otherness, evil, or one of its surrogates." Such pressures are psychic, social, and linguistic, and they are shot through with manifestations of
power.[18]

Connolly thus gives us the basis for a portrait of subjectivity and politics
that is both more agonistic than many modern, liberal ones and less unre-
lentingly antagonistic than the Schmittian alternative. But we need to fill out
that portrait of subjectivity further in order to see why such an individual
might be drawn to resist those persistent psychic, social, and linguistic pressures toward intensified antagonism in political life. In short, at this point we
have an ontology and politics that do not automatically make antagonism
our destiny, but we do not yet have an ethos of subjectivity that would give
sense and motivational force to our resistance to the very real pressures that
draw us toward that fate.

For the modern, disengaged subject, identity has typically not been a central problem. The *un*obtrusiveness of identity is crucial to envisioning life as
a self-controlled project initiated from a disengaged stance. The need to
maintain a smooth, secure sense of self demands that one quickly shuffle
aside experiences that call this stability into doubt, especially those that un-
dermine our urge to mastery of the world around us, as well as those that enhance the anxiety we feel about our finitude. In short, we treat being as if it
were designed to be endlessly pliant to our projects. But if we understand being, as Connolly does, as a persistent and never fully manageable presencing
of "identity\difference," then this imperious demand for security will appear
to be self-deceptive. As I previously noted, many social, linguistic, and psychic pressures feed this demand; and yet, if we embrace an ontology of a rich
and fugitive play of identity\difference, then simply conforming to these
pressures puts us deeply at odds with the character we have attributed to being. This relation of incongruence provides a reason to resist such pressures.
Of course, for that reason to carry any force for us, we must assume that we
prefer to imagine ourselves and our social world as in some sort of congruence, or attunement, with our deepest commitments regarding being. Such
an assumption does not seem to be implausible or unreasonable.

Having made this assumption, we would aim to conduct ourselves so as to
do justice to being, to more actively witness it, to put ourselves in a mimetic
relation to it. But in what spirit does one take up this task? Connolly would

have us experience the "nonteleological excess of being over identity" as a richness, or abundance; in Heidegger's terms, it is a "giving," the *Es gibt* of being.[19] When the originary energy and display of life is taken in this sense, it can evoke sentiments of reverence, enchantment, and gratitude. Now there is nothing certain about these sentiments; being does not guarantee them. To the contrary, one must cultivate them assiduously, for often that originary energy of presencing deals us hard blows; and, within Connolly's ontology, it is to these sentiments above all that one must look for sustenance at such times.

In our relations with others, such sentiments can manifest themselves as an ethos of "generosity and forbearance" toward that presencing of difference that continually unsettles one's identity. As was shown in the preceding chapter, Connolly speaks here of a "critical responsiveness," by which he means that one engages "the play of identities, institutions, and principles" with the aim of "rendering them more responsive to that which exceeds them, more generous and refined in their engagement with difference."[20]

Thus one can understand in a fuller sense both the cognitive and aesthetic-affective attraction of the disposition of presumptive generosity. And with that understanding, it becomes easier to see the plausibility of an orientation that is receptive to the critique of the modern, Western notion of subjectivity and yet also offers, as a positive alternative, a robust figure of subjectivity affirming a tempered agonistic picture of being.

II. Questioning the Critique

At this point, my claim would be that I have found a way of thinking in the aftermath of the critique of subjectivity that holds some promise. But this promise has been allowed to emerge only by assuming the essential legitimacy of the critique of subjectivity. There are, however, some problems with that assumption that must be confronted before one can feel any real confidence that such promise is not deceptive.

As I said earlier, the critique has understood itself to be an attack on liberalism. The legitimacy of this attack has, unsurprisingly, been contested by contemporary liberals in a variety of ways. In this section, I want to probe this dispute from the viewpoint of what seems to me the strongest liberal paladin in this fight, namely, political liberalism.[21] It maintains that, whatever the vulnerability of earlier forms of liberalism to critique, its own peculiar commitments render it invulnerable. If this is correct, then a view like Connolly's and mine must simply be based on false assertions about liberal subjectivity.

Recall the features of the modern subject upon which I have been focusing: disengagement; universally agreeable, rational principles of justice; and a conviction that the foregoing is founded on nature, God, progress, or the necessary normative core of ordinary language communication. The critics contend that the disengaged subject of the liberal tradition cannot adequately represent the agonism of political life rooted in the tensions of identity and difference. And this inadequacy encourages a propensity to overestimate the ease with which universally valid principles can be generated. Finally, it is argued that such principles have traditionally been rooted in foundationalist premises that are no longer convincing.

How do political liberals respond? They counter, first, that their framework does, in its own way, come to terms with the agonistic quality of political life. As we saw in Chapter 2, political liberalism begins with a central historical lesson of the late-modern world: we must accept "reasonable pluralism" or "reasonable disagreement" between "comprehensive conceptions of the good."[22] In short, we have learned that tension and deep disagreement between different views of the good life do not tend toward any clear telos of reconciliation. Second, political liberalism can demonstrate that the validity of the principles of a neutral, constitutional state is warranted not by any strong ontological foundation, but instead by political agreement between subjects who remain nevertheless in a condition of reasonable disagreement regarding their views of the good. This, in short, is the political liberal's narrative for how we get from antagonism to agonism and agreement.

What sort of subject can recognize himself in this narrative of political liberalism? In Chapter 2, I showed how Larmore argues persuasively that Rawls's model works only if we assume that subjects accord each other equal respect. And they will do this only if they affirm an ontology within which each human possesses a peculiar dignity. When such a minimal moral ontology is in place, one can plausibly project oneself into a narrative in which actors resist the temptation to script others into roles that mark them as warranting hostility or denigration. In this section, I look more closely into this matter of political liberalism and otherness, and argue that the foregoing resolution of it is only apparent. Although I will thus find political liberalism wanting, its emphasis on the core value of respect remains important to my conception of a late-modern ethos. I indicated this agreement already in Chapter 2, but I have not yet illuminated the specific role it plays in such an ethos. I will turn to that task in the next section.

Larmore argues that political liberalism can justly accommodate deep disagreement only if we admit that it tacitly accords a central role to the value of equal respect. And, for it to play this role, it must be part of an ontological framework in which each individual is imagined as having a distinct kind of dignity. Characterizations of dignity have traditionally taken the form of asserting that individuals have some peculiar quality that elevates them above the rest of the natural world. When I see the other human as elevated in this way, the appropriate aesthetic-affective reaction is, as Kant said, a feeling of the sublime *(die Erhabene)*.[23] This feeling is induced when one confronts something grand, immense, grave, potentially threatening, or painful.[24] Kant sees human beings as possessing these qualities when they are envisioned as free and rational creatures of the "noumenal" world. Entities in that world loom above humans considered only as creatures of the natural world.[25] Of course, the crucial character of elevation can be interpreted in ways other than Kant's rather peculiar one. More familiar in the West are the variants that lend humans elevation directly from God. This sort of ontological figuration can be seen in quarters as diverse as John Locke in the seventeenth century and Eleanor Roosevelt in the twentieth. In the latter's thought (distinctively important given her central role in the writing of the UN Declaration of Human Rights in 1948), we see human beings elevated by the gift of a divine "spark"; in Locke's thought, we are accorded the status of agents of God: humans are "sent into the world by his order, and about his business; they are his property, whose workmanship they are, made to last during his, not one another's pleasure."[26]

But Larmore does not want to load political liberalism up with any more ontological baggage than necessary; accordingly, he avoids weighty figures like God or noumenal realms. Human dignity rests for him on what makes humans the natural wonders of *this* world; namely, their "capacity for working out a coherent view of the world."[27] We are grand because we are *capacious:* we reason freely and bring new order into the world. It is before the dignity of this being that we are moved to show respect. And it is this movement that holds in check the temptation/pressure to react with hostility toward the other, and thus accommodate persistent, deep difference, which, in turn, is crucial to our progress toward agreement about the basics of a just society.

I want to argue, however, that this portrait of a minimalist normative foundation for political liberalism is not as felicitous as Larmore believes.[28] For present purposes, I will concede that he provides us with a persuasive sequence of reasons for establishing agreement on just basic structures; nevertheless, these structures will be at risk of being inadequately supplied with motivations on the part of citizens unless this portrait is changed so as to have a better comprehension of the pervasiveness of agonism, as well as of the aesthetic-affective and moral resources necessary to effectively engage that agonism. At bottom, I will be claiming that the basic structures of a just society will be more likely to maintain their justness over time if we imagine that reproduction being mediated by a late-modern ethos with a somewhat thicker moral core and a greater attention to agonism than is the case in Larmore's account.

When we properly understand dignity and respect, according to Larmore, our rational reflections move us clearly toward the affirmation of some variant of liberal principles of justice. I don't want to contest this train of argument head-on but, rather, linger somewhat longer than he does at his figuration of the moral-ontological core of the construct. More specifically, I want to think more carefully about the aesthetic-affective disposition that is engendered in such a core. One might immediately object here that a core like Larmore's—with its strong Kantian flavor—will not be dependent on any aesthetic-affective elements. But that is not actually the case even with Kant himself, as I began to show a moment ago. Although he did wish to keep his logic of pure practical reason separated from any aesthetic-affective commitments, he nevertheless felt compelled to refer to that sentiment of the sublime that we experience when faced with an other who is apprehended as bearing that dignity of a free and rational being. Now it may have been important to Kant to try to keep the image of such an entity above the natural, phenomenal world, in which we are partially motivated by affect, but philosophers today typically do not buy into a noumenal/phenomenal distinction and thus have no comparable reason to refrain from more careful attention to aesthetic-affective considerations.

Surprisingly little has been said about such matters in the case of the value of equal respect. Today, respect seems to be such a self-evident good that we don't really have to think much about it. It has a kind of positive default role in regard to the terrain of moral-political reflection. The logic it implicitly warrants could be described in the following way: If actors show respect to one another, then everyone's rights remain intact, and consequently we must already be a good part of the way toward whatever legitimate framework of cooperation might be possible. What more could one citizen expect from another?

But perhaps respect is not quite the value for all seasons we think it is. In the present context, I want to suggest that respect may not, by itself, be enough of a moral core, at least when it comes to a late-modern account of justice such as political liberalism understands itself to be. Let me start this line of reflection by considering very specifically how, within the liberal Kantian tradition, a subject is disposed toward an object of respect. The word that Kant used, that we translate as "respect," is *Achtung*.[29] *Achtung* is typically used in everyday life as something like a warning or a call to be wary or at least extra attentive. Further, *attentive* here means "attentive to my own well-being" and *wary* means "recognizing the possibility of some threat I may have to face" (and this fits how the sublime is associated with the potential for some sort of pain or harm that I might suffer).

The question to pose is whether the subject imagined here as backing away from the other in an attitude of disengagement offers a plausible figure in terms of which to grapple with the problem of agonism. Respect is a kind of rough-cut, partially self-regarding, giving-of-space to the other. Clearly such a figure of space-creation is important in some ways in accommodating the agonistic character of social life; it subtends, for example, the virtue of tolerance. But does it consistently and attentively engage that temptation/pressure to script what is different into a multitude of hostile roles? Respect is, as it were, an official attitude in the liberal state, in terms of which the structure of basic laws and institutions can be comprehended. But the question here is whether it adequately animates the everyday "choices . . . that people make *within* such institutions."[30]

We can certainly see respect embodied in some sorts of everyday choices that citizens of politically liberal polities would make. Just as respect inspires constitutional laws that enshrine the value of tolerance in our basic texts, so one would expect that people would also show tolerance in everyday life, thereby continually affirming the basic value of respect. The ontology of subjectivity in political liberalism brings tolerance to life vis-à-vis the other's identity, here portrayed as fixed in character, in relation to which I honor the value of respect through the exercise of tolerance.[31] But such a world of beings with fixed identities moving around—or in this case away from—each other, does not catch the distinctive dynamic element of agonism as it appears in either Schmitt or Connolly. For us to do justice to agonism, we need an ontological picture of identity and difference as constitutively entwined and a congruent psychological-political picture of actors who continually face the temptation/pressure to transform difference into otherness. Compare here the array of ontological figures and aesthetic-affective and moral dispositions that Connolly offers with the ones we have just found to be associated with political liberalism. His subject acknowledges its constitutive dependence on, or indebtedness to, difference and the temptation/pressure that is implicit in it for anxious, mortal beings. And the primary way in which this is acknowledged is by a persistent cultivation of a presumptive generosity toward the other. Understood in this fashion, generosity has two aspects. First, it has a quality of initial openness and attentiveness toward difference that *bears witness* to, or *expresses a mimetic relation* with, the agonistic becoming or presencing of life. And, second, it *dampens the persistent temptation* to transform difference into hostile otherness.

At this point, the political liberal might decide in self-defense that although she wants to affirm some degree of agonism as implicit in her portrait of a pluralistic world, she can safely refuse what she sees as a turn to a more robust and intransigent agonism favored by critics of liberal subjectivity. Although I think good grounds exist for such a strategy in relation to a Schmittian agonism, the same does not hold true for the kind that Connolly and I would affirm.

When it comes to our most basic weak-ontological formulations of something like the kind and degree of agonism we imagine in the world, there are of course no drop-dead arguments with which we can target an opponent. But this does not mean there are no arguments. As I have portrayed her, the political liberal would refuse to see the world as more robustly agonistic, because to do so would involve importing into her moral core additional virtues beyond respect; more particularly, presumptive generosity. And, if she were to do that, then perhaps the likelihood of finding a universally valid, substantive, overlapping consensus on justice of the Rawlsian sort might be reduced. This outcome is indeed a possible cost of assuming a more robust agonism. However, not making this assumption entails costs as well. Rawls, as I noted earlier, bases his political conception of justice on the historical lesson of recurring conflict from early modern times to today. But surely there can be different ways of interpreting exactly what the lesson involves and how we can best respond. In Chapter 2, I referred to J. S. Mill's appeal to something like an ethos when he argued that the problem of cultivating tolerance in one's own thinking and visceral reactions was more than a matter of obeying laws. Mill's claims here reflect his reading of a historical lesson about the deep and recurring dangers of intolerance. What sort of assumption does Mill make about tolerance and intolerance as a result of taking this lesson to heart? He decides to assume that intolerance is "natural to mankind . . . in whatever they really care about."[32] Now this assumption is quite interesting, given how Mill, in *On Liberty,* eschews the strategy of using the idea of "the natural" to help justify basic claims about central values like rights.[33] If Mill were to have been confronted with the curious character of his assumption that intolerance is natural, I think he would have answered along the following lines. We certainly cannot validly conclude that intolerance is natural directly from a reading of the historical record. But, given the prevalence and persistence of intolerance in history, as well as our affirmation of the primacy of individual freedom, perhaps we would be wise to make a somewhat hyperbolic assumption about such matters; that is, in order to heighten our vigilance against intolerance, we might construct a story of ourselves that buries this propensity deep in our "natures."

My suggestion would be that we might want to think in an analogous way about agonism. Modern Western political thought has continually shown itself to be susceptible to an overly optimistic, rationalist universalism that masks and downplays very real bases of legitimate political struggle. If we do indeed care about enhancing freedom, equality, and democratic inclusion, then perhaps we would be well advised to begin to reimagine ourselves and our world—even at the cost of a certain hyperbole—in a more robustly agonistic fashion.

III. A Late-Modern Subject

The preceding argument for the significance of a presumptive generosity should not be understood to imply a demotion in significance of the value of equal respect. Both are equally crucial in a portrait of late-modern subjectivity that does justice to the key dimension of agonism and the problems it generates for ethical-political life. However, some late-modern thinkers, including Connolly, manifest a tendency—at least implicitly—to allow respect to slide into something of a secondary position in relation to generosity. The relative lack of concern about this outcome arises from misgivings about the way the object of respect is often defined in the modern, liberal tradition. (I am referring here to secular or nontheistic variants within this tradition. In the next chapter, I bring theistic ones into the discussion.) The individual is taken by this tradition to be the bearer of a dignity whose qualities are generally enumerated in a fashion similar to what we found in Larmore: that is, as a kind of capaciousness conceived in terms of the exercise of freedom and reason. For Connolly, this tradition has tended to allow capaciousness to take on the form of a persistent orientation toward the mastery or normalization of the other.[34] Human dignity thus ends up deeply compromised by its association with domination.

A liberal would likely take exception to this claim that his conception of human dignity has any such necessary association. Moreover, he might argue that without a figure of dignity that is of equal significance to the figure who responds to an agonistic world with generosity, one ends up with humans having no clear priority in relation to nonhuman nature. In short, there would be no ontological elevation whatsoever of the human. Would Connolly really want to affirm the consequences of this? A parade of horribles, as lawyers say, is easy to assemble. For example, imagine a country where one group faces the prospect of genocide at the hands of its enemy; and imagine as well that the associated fighting between the two sides threatens the habitat of a given species of bird to such a degree that it may go extinct. Would Connolly really be indifferent as to how he would rank the priority of courses of action that would save, respectively, that group of people or that nonhuman species?

I don't agree with Connolly's position here; but neither do I think the traditional modern argument about the priority of the human is adequate. Rather, I want to affirm a figure of subjectivity in which the two aspects, presumptive generosity and capacious dignity are equi-primordial. My strategy is to work on reconfiguring the features of human being that are most highlighted in the typical definition of capaciousness. Those who affirm the primacy of human capaciousness tend to define dignity with phrases such as "*form* and *revise* a *plan* of life," or "*work out* a *coherent* view of life." When

this type of capaciousness is stressed, it is not surprising that dignity often reduces to the potential for a kind of mastery or reflective planning project. But
suppose we redefine capaciousness as something such as "the meaning-
making of a meaning-seeking creature." This change enacts a crucial shift of
focus and substance but remains clearly within the range of what capaciousness connotes. First, when the "making" is now focused on meaning, it draws
our attention more to the fact that the medium of what is distinctly *human*
making is ordinary language and the articulation of ontological sources. That
capacity is brought to bear as we articulate the character of our ontological
sources under the challenge of new experience. When the linguistic character
of this activity is emphasized, so also is the sense that full articulacy is never
our fate. Our capaciousness does indeed mean that we can master much in
the world, but such projections always remain arrayed before a background
of remaining inarticulacy. As *capacious,* we are always also *captive* in this
sense.

This shift in the sense of capaciousness also allows for its becoming less
central in our understanding of human dignity. This modification can occur
because of the way inarticulacy not only reflects our being in ordinary language but also our limitations as mortals. The core of our character as
"meaning-seeking" creatures arises from the consciousness of our finitude,
our mortality. Ultimately, we worry about meaning, about having a plan of
life or view of the world because we are finite; we select from limited choices
and have a limited span of time to make sense of ourselves.[35] In short, if one
of the fundamental sources of ourselves is capaciousness, the other is our subjection to mortality. Once we comprehend this, the meaning of human dignity is modified significantly. I will provide a fuller treatment of how we
should understand human dignity in the next chapter. For the moment, my
point is that when we highlight human consciousness as a capacity, we need
to attend not just to the dimension of planning or potential mastery that
comes with this ontological figure but also to the anxiety of mortality that
quietly accompanies this capacity for natality.

When the dignity of the human subject is imagined in this fashion, there is
less reason to follow Connolly's implicit suggestion that we blur the dividing
line between the elevated position of human being and the rest of being. In
the alternative I am suggesting, the figure of the human subject should still
warrant a distinctive, though different, kind of elevation. And that, in turn,

should still evoke a distinctive feeling of sublimity. But now that feeling must be cultivated in relation to the sort of reflective insight I have developed about the overinflation of capaciousness. Burke suggested something similar when he distinguished between a "false sublime" and an authentic one. The former was evoked by the thrill of the imagined infinitude of human capacity.[36] For Burke, this danger was associated with an extreme case: the behavior of the Jacobins in the French Revolution. My concern about the liberal elevation of the capacious subject does not depend upon any facile equation of liberalism and Jacobinism. But the liberals' failure to fold a consciousness of mortality into their notion of subjectivity resonates with Burke's underlying point; namely, that an authentic feeling of the sublime is evoked by an object's uncanny juxtaposition of the exhilaration of something that is simultaneously grand but sobered by an association with death.

4

Animating the Reach of Our Moral Imagination

The fourth significant late-modern challenge to Western ethical-political thought has to do with how well that tradition can reenvision itself beyond the borders of the nation-state. Are our familiar ontological figures and basic concepts adequate for a world in which our attention is pushed more and more toward questions of global justice and human rights for those who live at great distances from us, in both a geographical and a cultural sense? In the preceding chapters, I have broached this broad topic indirectly in my discussion of problems that arise around the familiar liberal figure of the autonomous or capacious subject, and whether it draws us to engage adequately with the issues of agonism and difference that seem only to become more important as the processes of globalization become an ever-more prominent part of our lives.[1]

In this chapter, I want to press further in evaluating the wisdom of defining the core of human dignity only in terms of the capaciousness of crafting, following, and reconceiving a plan of life. At first glance, it might seem that this portrait of humans and the equal respect they owe each other would put one in a relatively favorable position when it comes to thinking about human rights and global justice. But, in fact, the liberal stance is rather more unstable in that regard than might be thought initially. To see this, one has to take seriously an aspect of being late-modern that I noted in the Introduction, namely, the realization that an ethos of late modernity cannot blithely assume that theistic arguments are the immediate nonstarters many modern philosophers have taken them to be. Theists have traditionally argued that the line of thought linking the capacious subject to commitments to human rights and global justice is a deeply problematic one, once God is taken out of the picture. In other words, if the liberal constellation of dignity, equality, and respect arrayed around the value of autonomous agency is felicitous, then it possesses that quality only because of an *unacknowledged* theism that haunts its basic assumptions.

It is important to my project to consider this theistic challenge very carefully, both because late-modern thought generally needs to take religious views more seriously, and because my notion of an ethos and the figure of human dignity it embodies have to be configured in such a way that they do not repeat mistakes made by the contemporary nontheistic liberal. This means that for me to grapple adequately with the late-modern challenge of distance, I will need to start by confronting this theistic critique. Toward this end, the present chapter first elucidates in more detail the character of the theistic critique (Section I).[2] Second, I sketch some ways in which nontheistic liberals have tried to blunt the force of that critique (Section II). Each of these strategies is shown to be relatively ineffective. Finally, I introduce a kind of response to the theistic position that admits some of its force and yet remains nontheistic (Section III). This response involves a refiguration of human being that makes it less *unbalanced*; that is, less exclusively focused on the powers and capacities of agency and more attentive to our subjection to mortality. As a result of this refiguration, it should become clearer why a late-modern ethos and the particular constellation of dignity, equality, and respect that animate it provide a perspective and sensibility that foster, in turn, an ethical imagination that is more easily extended across great distances than is the more familiar, secular liberal one.

I. The Theistic Critique

Quite often in the past, the nontheistic liberal has treated the religious critique as simply not very challenging. A fully adequate answer to that critique, it is assumed, can be found in a variety of philosophical sources. In fact, the real problem should be seen rather as lying with the theist for her dogged refusal to admit the cogency of the nontheistic position. The difficulty comes down to the failure of the theist to be tolerant. As David Hollinger writes: "If the religious are to be granted their Yahweh and their Christ, their Ten Commandments and their Sermon on the Mount, then we secularists should be allowed our Locke and our Rousseau, our Dewey and our Habermas, our Thomas Jefferson and our Elizabeth Cady Stanton."[3]

The fact that Locke stands at the front of this line of philosophical sources of contemporary liberalism is not surprising. His powerful case for individual rights and freedom makes him one of the most eminent of liberalism's founding fathers. Of course, Locke himself believed that such rights were rooted in God's moral order. But this fact has not daunted secular liberals. They have found it relatively easy to assume that the ideas of freedom and rights can be pried loose from their theistic foundation. The operative assumption is that freedom and rights are necessary for the protection and flourishing of human agency. The capacity for such agency—that is, the capacity to frame and potentially revise a life plan—is what raises us up over the rest of nature and, thus, what gives to human life its unique dignity. And it is on the basis of the respect that is owed equally to such creatures that one accords them rights. In short, the pivotal moment of sublimity that brings the self up short before the other has an adequate secular substitute. It is the grandeur of agency per se that is substituted for the elevated stature of a creature who is God's agent, who is, as Locke puts it, "sent into the World by His order and about His business."[4] But does this substitution in fact work as successfully as the nontheist imagines? Recently, Jeremy Waldron has argued that, in fact, it does not work.[5] Waldron focuses upon the equality part of the constellation of dignity, equality, and respect. Within the nontheist's argument, equality is often taken to be the easiest value to establish. Consider how quickly this whole issue is laid to rest by Jack Donnelly, a prominent theorist of human rights: "Human rights are *equal* rights: one either is or is not a human being, and therefore has the same rights as everyone else (or none at all)."[6] What Waldron shows is that this kind of quick conclusion is not really persuasive. It has to establish not only the threshold for what counts as human being, but also why differences in humans *above* that threshold are really not of much significance compared to that of simply being *over* the threshold.[7] In short, one has to be able, first, to identify some property that establishes that being's initial claim to equal treatment; and then, second, to show that differences in the possession of that property *above* the threshold do not warrant claims to inequality.

For Locke, humans are morally equal by virtue of possessing reason in the sense of a minimal capacity for abstraction. This threshold simply delineates the capacity to reason from the fact of my existence back to three necessary conclusions: first, that God created the world; second, that each individual is thus his subject or servant "about His business"; and, third, that each accordingly is bound to respect the right of all to go about that business unharmed. For Locke, all adult humans are capable of *this* sort of reason; and thus they are morally equal. Differences *beyond* this basic competence are morally irrelevant, however much they might be relevant in other ways.

So, in Locke, each individual's reflection on the meaning of his existence discovers God and his status as his subject bound to respect his order. By contrast, the individual as imagined by the nontheistic liberal finds through reflection only herself as a being who can in fact reflect upon herself and her choices; that is, who has the power, or capacity, to frame and revise her plan of life. In Locke's case, the moral significance of reason is that it allows you to understand your obligation as a subject; in the liberal's case, reason's significance is that it allows you to comprehend that you have the power to direct your life. The problem for the latter is that this power, or capacity, of practical reasoning can vary rather dramatically between individuals. And if this is so, shouldn't our assessment of the dignity and moral worth of individuals vary accordingly? Here the nontheistic liberal has no argument against the basic inequality of human beings.

Waldron's specific challenge to the nontheist concerning basic equality is perhaps best understood as contributing to a more general challenge that has received its most effective formulation from Charles Taylor, at the end of his *Sources of the Self*.[8] The standard liberal constellation of dignity, equality, respect, and capacious agency is typically connected to very high, universal moral standards. But Taylor doubts whether these values can adequately sustain such exacting standards. As he says, "high standards need strong sources."[9] When our sources reduce simply to an affirmation of agency, we don't get the same sort of cognitive and affective power in our sense of obligation that Christianity provides through its notion of our duty to participate in a divinely rooted love—in the sense of *agape*—as we engage the other. The standard liberal position condenses the dignity of human being into the figure of the agent without the "positive underpinning" of a persisting "affirmation of being."[10] We nontheists do owe the other agent respect, but this way of imagining the initial connectedness of human beings reduces to the bald imperative to back away from the other and his projects.[11] This is, by itself, not an effective enough source of connectedness. It embodies nothing that enlivens the sort of ethos of attentiveness and concern for the other that might effectively coax our moral imagination across cultural and geographic borders. Without this sort of underlying affirmation, our respect for the other's dignity or worth is deeply susceptible to disappointment, frustration, and resentment, dispositions that can easily slide toward feelings of hostility.[12]

II. Liberal Response

What sort of responses to the foregoing theistic arguments can the liberal offer? I will consider two types. First, there are those that tell us we should not take the theist's bait but, rather, simply change the subject (A). Second, there are those that take up the challenge more or less directly (B).

A. Avoiding the Theistic Critique

The theistic critique rests on some sort of appeal to ultimate or beyond-human foundations. One way liberals deal with such claims is by effectively changing the subject at issue. A popular variant of this strategy is to turn the charge of foundational deficit back onto the theist in the form of a charge that theistic foundations have promoted substantial violations of human rights in the past.[13] Now the issue becomes one of choosing between being ontologically unclear but tolerant, on the one hand, and being prone to dressing up horrible abuses in the mantle of transcendent truth, on the other. The theist now will have something to worry about that should weigh more heavily upon her than the mere problem of uncertain foundations that the liberal must bear.

This argument can be paired with another that also increases the relative attractiveness of the nontheistic liberal's position. Worries about unclear foundations can simply be bracketed off and ignored for present purposes; we need to focus instead on the rather large areas of agreement that actually already exist (about, for example, torture) around the globe among peoples with very different foundational commitments.[14] The agenda of global justice is best advanced by not worrying too much about which foundation is ultimately more adequate, but rather by seeking out areas of "overlapping consensus" around which a more robust human rights regime can be slowly constructed.[15]

How effective are these strategies for shifting attention away from the work of articulating foundations? It seems to me that they are both partially effective. Proponents of religiously based foundations should certainly be reminded that such a mode of justification has been used, and still is used, to warrant human rights violations. Similarly, it is indeed unwise to press questions that expose foundational disputes when actual cooperation can otherwise be achieved regarding concrete measures to reduce specific assaults on human rights.

However, even if one admits the good sense of such strategies, that does not by itself deny the importance of articulating the character of one's foundations. It merely tells us we need to think in a variety of ways about both how and when we should reflect on our foundations, and how we should always be open to pragmatic options that effectively restrain clear rights violations. Nevertheless, even after we have admitted that there are multiple possible foundations for thinking about human rights, and we have become sensitized to the value of not always highlighting the points at which different foundations conflict with one another, we still are faced with persistent questions about the clarity and coherence of the most basic affirmations that animate our moral-political reflections, judgments, and actions.

The exchange that takes place in Michael Ignatieff's volume on *Human Rights as Politics and Idolatry* is instructive in this regard. In his lectures, Ignatieff initially tries to work out an approach that avoids all foundational claims, and rather appeals straightforwardly and exclusively to the value of human agency and the crucial but instrumental role that human rights play in protecting it. This minimal, pragmatic appeal renounces any foundational talk about "the dignity of each human being" or "ultimate respect."[16] Ignatieff's intention is to develop a justification of human rights that continually directs us to look at every violation of rights in terms of specific remedies that should be developed and implemented on the basis of a savvy political awareness of the bounds of what is doable at any given time and place.

Again, there is much to admire in an effort such as this that seeks to avoid the "idolatry" of human rights, whether this reverence emerges from a religious or secular faith. But in his response to critics, Ignatieff finds himself forced to revise his position, now admitting that rights talk unavoidably depends, in one way or another, upon "deeper vocabularies" of ontological figuration and moral orientation that circulate around concepts such as human dignity and equality.[17] Thus Ignatieff ultimately grants that even his common sense, pragmatic approach to human rights ends up entangled in the need for more sustained reflection upon foundations than he at first thought. He concludes by affirming what might be called the liberal's default position: one acknowledges the need to engage the idea of dignity, but one reduces it simply to the figure of capacious agency. And yet does this affirmation of "dignity as agency" not put Ignatieff right back in the sort of position that Waldron and Taylor have effectively criticized?[18] The general moral of this story, the theist would argue, is that once one gets pushed to this foundational level, his arguments look quite strong compared to those of the nontheistic liberal.[19]

B. Engaging the Theistic Critique

So far, I have tried, first, to give some sense of the propensity of nontheistic liberals to meet the theist's challenge by simply avoiding it through one means or the other; and, second, to indicate that this strategy does not work quite so easily as its proponents sometimes think. In this section, I want to examine another liberal strategy. This one employs the notion of "overlapping consensus" to some degree, but it also frankly recognizes the limits of such efforts at avoidance and thus the necessity of directly engaging the theist's challenge regarding foundations.

The strategy of seeking an overlapping consensus is, of course, associated with Rawls and the structure of his argument for "political liberalism." Rawls asserts that we can arrive at appropriate principles of justice if we simply agree to be "reasonable" in our deliberations and seek an agreement that each party can affirm without his or her comprehensive, foundational commitments being brought into the discussions.[20] Although Rawls's recourse to overlapping consensus emerged first in his theory of justice within nation-states rather than in the global context of human rights claims, he and others deploy the notion of such a consensus in this latter context as well.[21] Larmore's political liberalism is particularly interesting in the present context; although he affirms the notion of overlapping consensus in general, he does not think that it is quite as successful as most political liberals believe in thoroughly insulating reflections on justice (domestic or global) from entanglement with moral foundations.

As we saw in Chapters 2 and 3, Larmore tries to defend political liberalism while admitting that its assumption of reasonableness implies that parties to the overlapping consensus affirm a foundational equal respect for one another. What is especially significant here is what he says about the grounds for according each person basic respect. Such respect, he contends, "cannot be easily separated from the religious traditions that gave it birth." In short, he shares Taylor's "suspicion" that the moral sources of the modern liberal self may be essentially religious in nature.[22] Larmore's surprising admission is followed, however, by the claim that the apparent victory of the theist here is, in fact, only that—apparent. The reason for this is that if it is acknowledged that we modern secular liberals' fundamental belief in human dignity and respect is founded upon theistic commitments that no longer have universal validity, does this not in itself throw that belief into doubt? This is the case, Larmore argues, because we do not stand under any obligation to justify a belief unless "some positive reason has arisen for us to doubt its truth." Thus, if we have no such reason to doubt our belief in human dignity and basic respect, then we need have no worry about the justifiability of its foundations. "Justification is required, not so much for belief itself, as for a change in belief."[23]

In sum, Larmore admits that the theist may be pointing out something significant about political liberalism; namely, that what authorizes its most basic beliefs in dignity and equal respect are even more basic, religious beliefs that many people today no longer share. But this situation does not require political liberals to admit defeat, because there is today no pressing reason for them to doubt modern democracy's standing commitment to dignity and equal respect.[24]

I want to suggest that Larmore's distinctive strategy for insulating political liberalism from the theistic challenge is more vulnerable than he thinks. Consider here the scandal in 2004, growing out of revelations concerning the abuse, torture, and murder of Iraqi prisoners held by the U.S. occupation forces in that country.[25] How should one interpret the significance of these occurrences for the self-understanding of America? It is hardly surprising that the administration of President George W. Bush and some military leaders immediately looked for ways to downplay the implications of this whole matter. Bush made it crystal clear that what was at issue were isolated actions for which a "few people" were responsible.[26] In effect, the problem was one of "a few bad apples." But this explanation simply ignores considerable evidence indicating the involvement of substantial numbers of military and civilian personnel, both high and low, and making clear that the mistreatment of prisoners was not confined to one prison facility or even one country, but rather seems to be a more general problem in this era of a continual "war on terror."

My suspicion is that if you asked those involved in one way or another in this mistreatment, most, if not all, would say that they believe in human rights and the notions of dignity and equal respect that support them. But somehow, in a specific set of circumstances, they arrived at justifications and engaged in practices that run counter to those commitments. If this is so, then the questions about prisoner abuse begin to take on a different and more disturbing color. Would a randomly selected U.S. citizen have likely behaved in the same way as those actually involved in the abuse? If she might have behaved similarly, does that perhaps say something unsettling about the relation between our general, abstract moral beliefs and the behavior that is supposed to instantiate them? Public opinion research in the United States over many decades has found substantial gaps between the almost unanimous support for a basic right such as freedom of speech when individuals are asked to give "yes" or "no" answers to a general question, on the one hand, and substantially less support when the same individuals are asked about support for affording that right in specific circumstances to a particular group toward whom there is a good deal of hostility, on the other hand.[27] All I wish to suggest here is that quite probing questions about basic values such as human dignity and equal respect and about the sources of their authority for us may be much more in order today than Larmore thinks.

Now Larmore might object that I have misconstrued what is at issue in the torture allegations. We don't need to ask basic, justificatory questions here; rather we need only condemn the individual soldiers for their blatant hypocrisy. They believe in human rights, but they fail to act in accordance with that belief. Such an objection, however, makes things too simple and tidy. Surely there is a question of ongoing moral-political education here that has to be broached. If this is true, however, I cannot see how the ensuing discourse could avoid the topic of why the protection of human rights is so fundamental to us. And once we are on this terrain, then the theist's challenge for secular liberals remains very much within the bounds of reasonable discussion.

It is important to be precise about what I mean here. I am not saying that the theist has an unassailable position in this discussion. In fact, my suspicion is that President Bush's particular religious views, which he interpreted as warranting continual talk about our "struggle against evil," helped create the sort of dehumanized perception of our enemy that, in turn, tacitly encouraged other Americans not to understand their own perceptions and actions as being in conflict with their abstract, general commitment to dignity and respect.[28] Again, my overall point is simply to say that reflection on the deepest level of our moral sources would seem to be warranted to a far greater degree than Larmore thinks.

III. A Nontheistic Ontological Figuration

If what I have said so far is correct, then arguments that place God in the constellation of dignity, equality, and respect are not so easy to ignore or knock down as nontheists have tended to imagine. The challenge is simply more fundamental and less easily answered than the liberals I surveyed in the preceding section admit. If this is so, what general standards would nontheists have to meet to respond more effectively to this challenge than they have up to now?

There seem to me to be two general standards to meet. First, one needs an ontological portrait of human being, the beyond human, and the core constellation of dignity, equality, and respect that does not involve God and yet can figure persuasively a sense of *limits upon agents* that functions comparably to the theistically based one that Waldron shows is operating within Locke. Second, this portrait must provide some way of figuring the *connectedness of agents* that functions comparably to the connectedness that Taylor says comes from the Christian belief that the individual should participate in the divine affirmation of human beings by loving humanity.

In what follows, I attempt to provide a sense of how the nontheist might meet these challenges. Toward that end, I first elaborate the notion of being "in subjection to mortality" and what it means to conceptualize this condition in weak ontological terms (A). Here I pick up and develop further the connection of mortality and dignity I touched upon at the end of Chapter 3. It is by vivifying consciousness of my subjection to mortality that I satisfy the attentiveness criterion of "being reasonable" in this space of the moral imagination of distant others. Second, I assess how well this notion of subjection to mortality allows us to figure limits upon agents and the character of their connectedness (B). This understanding of connectedness and limits satisfies the second criterion of reasonableness: self-restraint or self-imposed limits.

A. Being in Subjection to Mortality

When God is in the constellation of dignity, equality, and respect, one has a distinctive way of seeing how each agent, because of his equal reasoning capacity, can comprehend the natural law limitations on behavior. The dignity of each agent as a creature of God must be respected equally. And natural law sets out the specific limits that ought to constrain each agent.

The task for the nontheist is to find a way of figuring something comparable to this construction of equality and authoritative will so that each agent can see that she ought to restrain her behavior toward others. The difficulty of this task is pretty evident: without the authority of God, one merely has agency and, as Waldron has shown, it is not clear how one delineates a sense of the basic equality of individuals around which a sense of moral limitation might be constructed. What one needs, in brief, is something comparable to the equal capacity to reason from mere existence to the idea of a God who created human beings for a purpose. The specific problem for the nontheist is that when one tries to settle on some central human capacity or power in terms of which to frame basic equality and limitation, it is difficult to find a candidate that can successfully fill this role. As I indicated in Section II, Waldron shows us that without God in the constellation, it is not at all evident how we could isolate a particular characteristic of human beings and point to that as precisely the one that anchors our equality. The nontheist may think he can root equality in, say, the human capacity of reason, "but he will be at a loss to explain why we should ignore the evident differences in people's rationality. He will be at a loss to defend any particular line or threshold [that could determine the bounds of equality], in a non-question-begging way."[29] In sum, there seems to be no characteristic of agency that can authoritatively frame the individual as "subject to" in a way analogous to how the individual is framed as subject to God within the theistic perspective.

In wrestling with this problem, the nontheist might consider Thomas Hobbes's strategy. Just as in Locke's thought, in Hobbes's there is a "range property" in relation to which each individual is "in subjection." In the latter's state of nature, one exists not in equal subjection to God's order, but rather in equal subjection to the threat of violent death from one another.[30] In effect, each is equal enough in bodily strength that, through one means or another, each is a potentially deadly threat to any other. But if Hobbes provides us with a "range property" of human agency comparable in one sense to Locke's, in another sense Hobbes's property also illustrates precisely the difficulty to which I wish to call attention. Hobbes wanted individuals to comprehend how equal liability to violent death should cause each to constrain his reasoning in such a way that a political order of a certain sort is instituted. But equal subjection to the threat of violent death by itself engenders no moral limit on an individual, only a prudential limit that can be suspended whenever an individual finds it in his interest to do so. It makes perfect sense—as rational-choice theorists discovered many years ago—to free ride on any restraints that individuals might have agreed to. Thus the Hobbesian "subjection to" engenders neither the kind of limit upon agency nor the connectedness of agents that we need.

Nevertheless, Hobbes guides our attention in a promising direction: toward mortality. Perhaps the desired range value can be gotten from reflecting upon mortality, but in a somewhat different way: not as the violent death with which we can equally threaten each other but rather simply as the death to which we are all inescapably subject. Each of us is equal by virtue of the fact that we share the consciousness or foreknowledge that we will die.

I employ the expression "subjection to death" with the conscious intention of highlighting how alien this line of thought is to the liberal tradition today. Talk of *subjects* and *subjection* typically connotes a world of overbearing rulers and their obedient followers—exactly what Locke was beginning to free us from. The subjection I am referring to now is not subjection to a powerful *will*, be it that of a ruler or God, but rather to a *condition.*[31] And yet even in this form, it represents an unwelcome element within the modern, nontheistic liberal's ontology. For that tradition, as I noted earlier, the dignity of the human frequently coheres around the ontological figure of the capacious agent who has elevated herself above the rest of nature by choosing and pursuing a path through the world. The roots of this modern figure of dignity lie in the work of early Italian Renaissance writers who were consciously trying to overcome what they felt was a one-sided emphasis on the lowly condition of humankind in Christianity. Against the emphasis on the miserable, sinful, and mortal condition of human being, these writers saw themselves as involved in a rebalancing effort aimed at encouraging a sense of greater elevation.[32] Thus, any talk today of orienting the ontological figure of human being more around its subjection to mortality is likely to be perceived by nontheistic liberals as a deeply threatening gesture.

One way of thinking about the challenge of late modernity in the West is to see ourselves as confronted with our own problem of imbalance, only in reverse. This is certainly the way some religions see the present. My intention is to try to take this question of imbalance seriously, but without making theism the only option. The goal is to see if one can make sense of subjection to mortality in a way that reconceives and displaces somewhat the figure of the capacious agent without thereby simply denigrating it.

Agency constituted solely in terms of its powers to frame a life plan has, as its primary orientation to the world, a disposition to encounter all entities as potentially manageable material. For my purposes, such a disposition is problematic; but it should nevertheless not be seen solely in a negative light. As Ignatieff rightly notes, when we orient the constellation of dignity, equality, and respect around the figure of the capacious agent, we enact a deeply significant shift in our categorization of others, especially those who are in dire need. This shift disposes us to see those others as "rights-bearers" rather than as "the dependent beneficiaries of our moral concern." In other words, the figure of capacious agency is part of the necessary ontological infrastructure of a political world where each is to count as an "empowered" claimant.[33]

What is problematic about this otherwise admirable portrait of agency, however, emerges in the critiques that Waldron and Taylor have offered. Without a range value like Locke's which provides restraints or a disposition that connects one human to another, the default disposition of the claiming, capacious agent is one that orients it to the world as material to be managed or guarded against so as to best facilitate its plan of life. How would this change if one were to conceive of agency as taking shape from not one, but two ontological sources around which we figure dignity; that is, if one were to think in terms not only of the remarkable powers and capacities displayed by human being but also in terms of its peculiar access to the fact of its mortality?

I want to frame this question in a way that draws heavily upon Taylor's account of practical reason, according to which our engagement with new situations calls upon our skills of interpretation and judgment that, in turn, progressively "articulate" our underlying "moral sources."[34] As we saw in Chapters 2 and 3, such articulation is never complete; and thus we are never in a position from which we can announce the achievement of full articulacy in regard to that source. But I am also deviating somewhat from Taylor's thinking in one significant way. I speak more neutrally of "ontological," rather than "moral," sources. I intend by this shift in terminology to highlight the notion that something may function like Taylor's sources but be more amorphous in terms of potential moral guidance. Thus subjection to mortality may function as an ontological source, but it does not have quite the sort of clear—if never crystal clear—moral implications of Taylor's theistic source.

The key question now becomes: How does one figure subjection to mortality as an ontological source that is both robust and yet in fruitful tension with that preeminent modern source, the capacious agent? It is not difficult to figure this source simply as robust; for example, one can identify it with those moments of intense dread of death, which everyone experiences from time to time. For the nontheist, these moments can be thoroughly debilitating, but they are typically soon squeezed aside by more affirmative experiences of agency. For a theist, these moments likely heighten the urgency with which one feels compelled to cling to and perhaps purify one's belief and its divine source.[35] But if one hopes to figure subjection to mortality in a way that more quietly and more persistently challenges the sovereign dignity of capacious agency without recourse to God, one needs to attend to mortality somewhat differently.

We might figure it less as that before which we stand momentarily in intense dread and more as a burden under which we continually struggle, and for which we seek a mode of comprehension that embeds the awareness of that struggle in our everyday life as a countervailing force to the momentum we draw from our sense of ourselves as capacious agents. The goal we imagine is one of living in a way that balances these two sources of ourselves. My allowing the sense of myself as capacious to effectively displace attentiveness to mortality now becomes an act of bad faith analogous to the one Albert Camus famously analyzed. In his essay, "The Myth of Sisyphus," Camus pondered the shape of a life that continually faced the insight that we are mortals in a world with no intrinsic meaning secured by a transcendent truth.[36] Camus had relatively little to say in this essay by way of a positive prescription; rather he was at pains to show that the choice of suicide is not an adequate solution to this challenge. Suicide is an inadequate solution because it fails to honor the initial terms of the problem by simply eliminating one of them.

One, in effect, flees from the problem instead of meeting it. The question of how we should live with the consciousness of a world without foundations cannot, in good conscience, be avoided in this fashion. It is only by grappling attentively and persistently with it that we bear witness to the terms of our existence and thereby display the peculiar, basic dignity of which only humans are capable.

What I am suggesting is that when we orient ourselves—consciously or unconsciously—exclusively around capacious agency as our only ontological source, we are implicitly enacting an avoidance strategy analogous to the one to which Camus calls our attention. In effect, we operatively forget one of the terms of our challenge: being consciously subject to death in a world without transcendent guarantees. To grapple adequately with this challenge, we need to embrace a response that is as quietly and persistently effective in vivifying our sense of finitude as all the routines and diversions of affluent, modern life are in directing our attention away from it.

Although not formulated explicitly as a response to this specific need, Connolly's figuration of being in a world without God is quite useful for present purposes. He figures being as a continual, never fully manageable, fugitive becoming or presencing. Within such a world, my particular identity as an agent emerges from multilayered processes of isolating certain qualities from the abundance of this becoming. The construction of identity is constitutively dependent upon what is different from the continual work-in-progress that I am and that can never quite get both feet sovereignly planted on the ground. Difference in this ontological sense means that every manifestation of my identity is enabled, disturbed, and compromised by that against which it stands out.[37] What is crucial about this ontological figuration is that it vividly portrays the finitude of all projections of identity. If identity is constitutively dependent on difference, then my agency cannot complete a portrait of itself and its projects as sovereignly free in the sense of being beyond dependence on that which it is not.

As I showed in Chapter 2, this general character of being stands in no small degree of tension with the persistent desire modern humans have for their specific identities to achieve untrammeled capaciousness. We find it too painful and unsettling to admit the full degree to which our identity is always already in debt to what is other to us. Therefore we are continually drawn to strategies of flight that deceptively promise to prove our sovereign capacity to remove ourselves from relations of dependence. We are indeed capable of fleeing any given, particular dependence. And such flight becomes increasingly easy in the conditions of an affluent, consumerist lifestyle, as I indicated previously.

This sort of pain and anxiety can also be assuaged by more aggressive strategies. These include the ways in which I script that which is other to me into roles that portray it as alien, threatening, dangerous, or evil; in other words, I define the other in ways that seek to essentialize it as what must be categorically guarded against, denigrated, and combated. This underlying propensity toward a self-strengthening hostility is perhaps the most resilient and disturbing way in which we attempt to shore up the seductive image of ourselves as fully capacious agents. Such a self scripts its own identity as one always on the way to some conclusive resolution or clarification of a problem, some victory, revenge, or vindication, each of which in turn promises to keep us one step ahead of the need to come to better terms with our dependence.

Given this background, how might we rescript the self in a fashion that is effective in making clear the self-deception of sovereignty? Here one can begin to appreciate the peculiar quality of our foreknowledge of mortality, and how its vivification might have distinctive effects on the character of our thought and action in this domain. Subjection to mortality engenders a pain and anxiety from which one cannot flee with the same ease as is the case with the pain and anxiety arising from any given, normal relation of dependence on an other. It is far more difficult to construct a narrative for myself that denies my death than it is to construct one that portrays me as triumphing over some specific relation of dependence.

At this juncture, one can better comprehend the distinctive role that the consciousness of mortality can play in persistently interrupting that smooth imaginary of a sovereign self who continually sees itself as one step ahead of the constitutive entanglement of "identity\difference." When we allow the foreknowledge of mortality to have a persistent vividness in our life, it continually highlights the deception involved in the self-image of untrammeled capaciousness.

The task at hand is to reconfigure the pain and anxiety we feel in the face of our dependence on the other. In this reworking, our discomfort becomes the occasion not of immediate flight or hostility but rather of a more pervasive feeling of our mortality, our nonsovereignty. In short, our everyday experiences of finitude would be felt, at least partially, as persistent reminders of our mortality.[38] We would aim at interrupting and slackening the momentum of the self that would be sovereign. For this to happen, I would need to cultivate a cognitive and affective disposition that sustains a repertoire of ways of acting and reacting, continually bearing witness to, or gesturing toward, our mortality. This repertoire would function as a quiet, but ever-present, companion to the bold figure of capacious agency. One practice in this repertoire would certainly be the sort of presumptive generosity that I discussed earlier. Together, practices of this sort would form a central component of a late-modern ethos.

Before turning more directly to how the consciousness of mortality might inform the way we conceive of human connectedness and the problem of limits on capaciousness, I need to characterize this consciousness in more detail. A useful way to do so is by considering some objections that would likely be offered to what I have said so far. One objection to my focus on mortality might point to the disabling effect of my having begun the discussion by turning to Hobbes. The problem would be that the reflection on mortality that his actor undertakes is initiated from the perspective of a disengaged self. Yet this is clearly a perspective I have been arguing against throughout this book.

In response to this criticism, I would simply point out that my argument about mortality is not necessarily tied in any way to a Hobbesian portrait of disengagement. Although Hobbes was heuristically helpful in beginning to think about the issue of mortality, it makes better sense conceptually to imagine the genesis of reflection on finitude as occurring within an ontological scene of constitutive engagement of the self and other. Here I find Judith Butler's recent work quite helpful. The explicit focus of her discussion of the death of a loved other is somewhat different from mine. She is investigating different reactions—grief, rage, violence, mourning, and melancholy—to the experience of loss. There is nevertheless an implicit ontological claim in what she says that I would like to affirm. This claim is that one confronts mortality first through the death of the other. In other words, I do not sovereignly raise the subject of my own mortality; rather my sovereignty is "undone" (Butler's term) by the trauma of the loss of another. Thus I am always already thrown into the subject of mortality through my relation to others, regardless of my will.[39]

A second objection to my focus on finitude would contend that my effort to use the consciousness of mortality as a nontheistic, experiential basis for thinking about commonality and a minimal ethical orientation is too narrowly conceived and would be better formulated by attending to the general vulnerability to pain and suffering that all humans share. Bryan Turner has made a particularly careful and engaging defense of this relatively frequently heard argument.[40] He makes our "ontological vulnerability" the key to a universal sense of community that, in turn, "defines the common basis of human rights." This argument clearly relies on strong claims about how our openness to pain and suffering gives us a sense of our moral equality. As Turner says, "happiness is diverse, but misery is common and uniform." Against those who might try to argue that pain and suffering are culturally relative, Turner would admit that some psychological suffering might be culturally variable, but there is nevertheless some level at which brute, root commonality shines through: "a toothache is a toothache."[41] I suspect, however, that all such efforts to find a brute commonality rooted in pain and suffering will fail. In relation to Turner's example, one can easily see the unpersuasiveness of imagining a universal human bond around the common experience of something like a toothache. The problem for him is that, in fact, lots of people in the prosperous Western democracies have not had the experience of a serious toothache. I did not have one until I was fifty-seven, when a tooth had become infected and I could not get to a dentist—as I would normally—because of a long holiday weekend. I remember thinking at the time, as I writhed in pain: "*Now* I understand the significance of all those references to bad toothaches in history books and literature." (Obviously, those who live in poverty or without health insurance are likely to understand such references immediately.) My point here is that economic conditions and the level of health care render Turner's shared experiential ground far more variable than he thinks. Regarding toothaches, it would certainly be sensible (although perhaps a little strange) for me to say on my deathbed: "It was only because of bad luck that I did not make it to the end of my life without experiencing the terrible pain of a toothache." It would be rather more difficult to imagine myself saying: "It was only because of bad luck that I did not make it to the end of my life without becoming aware of my mortality."

In sum, mortality is different from our vulnerability to pain and suffering. This parallels Waldron's showing that, for Locke, our equal minimal capacity to reason back to a Creator is different from our more general capacity to reason that is clearly unequally distributed. The former, in both cases, can provide access to a distinctive sense of equality; the latter cannot, because of its variability among individuals.

When Turner enumerates the various characteristics of "ontological vulnerability," he does include death.[42] This inclusion is admirable, but it still confuses a central issue: mortality is not merely one more item on a list; rather it has a unique status vis-à-vis the other characteristics of vulnerability. Our consciousness of mortality is what gathers the other characteristics together in a field of meaning. Whatever else we make of given episodes of pain and suffering, they are always already moments that raise for us the problem of mortality. They are, in Burke's words, "emissaries" of our finitude.[43]

Another reason for skepticism of Turner's approach through the notion of general vulnerability is to consider possible undesirable implications of the categorical claim that "[v]ulnerability defines our humanity."[44] From the perspective I have been defending, Turner is correct to look for a way of defining humanity that is not exclusively tied to our capaciousness. However, if mortality is not given the distinctiveness I argue it deserves, one ends up with the figure of a human whose subjectivity forms—even if unintentionally—a smooth complement to an administrative-organizational gaze. What I mean by this can be grasped by attending to Turner's conception of human dignity. Interestingly, he says nothing directly about the ground of dignity, only that "suffering" constitutes "a loss of dignity."[45] This appears to allow for the demands of human dignity to be fully secured by organizational intervention aimed at relieving suffering. Now I am clearly pushing Turner in a direction he would not want to go; but from *within* his definition of human being, I do not see how he prevents this unfortunate slide. In short, Turner's approach to dignity makes us into what Ignatieff worries about: "dependent beneficiaries."[46] If one starts, however, with the subjection to mortality as the heart of human vulnerability, it is clear that no bureaucratic intervention is sufficient to relieve one of this condition in the same way that it might overcome the suffering caused by hunger and fear. No one can relieve me of my mortality (or at least not yet). They may provide material or psychological aid that is crucial, but this aid can only contribute to conditions under which I can pursue the reproduction of cultural life in a manner that I find best able to bear witness to my mortal condition.

There is one final direction from which my claims about mortality are open to skepticism. A critic might grant my point that humans share a consciousness of death in some unique, brute sort of way.[47] But this admission, it would be argued, can still be joined with a denial of my claim that such a shared consciousness gives us some distinctive ethical prefiguration. Here the critic would contend that the shared fact of death is always submerged in a field of cultural significance that gives death the specific meaning it has in a particular time and place. And the content of that field is highly variable. Some societies have practiced human sacrifice; others have affirmed suicide bombers who kill civilians; and still others—wealthy ones—have allowed poor people to die in great numbers in foreign countries, something that could be largely prevented with relatively little negative impact on the continuance of that affluence.[48]

There is no plausible way to deny this cultural and historical variability in the meaning of death. But the force of my argument does not actually depend on such a denial. I am not contending that mortality has a single, universal significance for all places and times. All I want to assert is that a vivified consciousness of mortality in late-modern Western democracies can have the sort of effect on ethical awareness that I have sketched. Such societies share two basic affirmations and one deep anxiety. They affirm the central value of the capacious individual in a universalizing way, and they are deeply committed to a future of continuing material progress as the best soil for the flourishing of that capaciousness. The source of anxiety in this context is the consciousness of mortality; it sits rather uncomfortably athwart the other two commitments. My claim that vivifying the consciousness of mortality may extend the reach of our imagination is conceived only against this sort of specific background.

B. Mortality, Limits, and Connectedness

Let me turn back now to the two deficits that I identified in nontheistic accounts of dignity, equality, and respect; namely, the lack of limits on the capacious agent and its ontological lack of any constitutive connectedness with other humans that is as deeply embodied as is the will to rationally pursue a plan of life. Looking first at the issue of limits, the question becomes the following: How might a late-modern ethos provide us with distinct limits to which we feel ourselves deeply obligated in a fashion that would parallel the dictates of Locke's natural law? In the latter case, each has equal dignity rooted in the elevated status of being in God's service. But in the nontheist's case, no such authoritative will provides that enhanced status that, in turn, is what makes me an object of a unique sort of respect.[49] My freedom as mortal agent encounters no externally grounded limits comparable to this obligation to respect all other agents who are upon God's business. All I have is the self-generated imperative to truthfully express the terms of my ontological condition. I will not to live a life that is self-deceptive, because that would conjure away, through one means or another, the full force of those terms. I see this sense of bearing witness truthfully to my condition of subjection to mortality as constituting the basis for the only sort of dignity that belongs uniquely to humans.

But it must be admitted that the kind of elevation that warrants this construal of dignity is achieved in the same way Baron von Munchhausen got himself out of the swamp into which he had fallen. In both cases, we merely need to grab ourselves by the hair and pull upwards. Is *this* a figuration of dignity? This sort of self-elevation appears at first almost comical, when contrasted with the Lockean agent whose elevation is leveraged by an omnipotent, external authority. This comical quality revolves around the impossibility of Munchhausen maneuvers in the physical world as well as in the realm of logic. But in the figuration of entities and ethe in a weak-ontological world, self-leveraging is a perfectly acceptable activity; one can cultivate or work on the self to move it from one state to another. In the present context, presumptive generosity, engaged at precisely those moments when one feels the "natural" urge to react defensively or with overt hostility toward that which seems to threaten the security of one's identity and rights, enacts just this sort of maneuver.

However, the difficulty of such self-leveraging or self-cultivation should not be underestimated, especially when that self's identity is construed largely as bearing rights that protect capaciousness. What Ignatieff refers to as the "empowerment" of such an agent might also be seen as a kind of "armament." The "bearing" of rights has connotations not unlike the "bearing" of arms. This self is heavily armored against all others. If this is so, such a weighty self is likely to be difficult to leverage by a disposition as diffuse and seemingly unnatural as an ethos of finitude. In sum, one would be well advised to retain a healthy degree of skepticism when it comes to imagining such an ethos as a fully effective source of limits upon the momentum of the rights-bearing, capacious self.

But perhaps the task could become more manageable if the notion of subjection to mortality could also be comprehended in such a way that a distinctive sense of human connectedness could be drawn out of it; in short, something that could function in a way that is analogous to the connectedness embodied in the notion of *agape*. When the sense of the basic equality of human beings takes its shape neither from God nor from pure agency, but rather from our subjection to mortality, I want to suggest that it offers a foothold for a subtle sense of community.

This would be a connectedness arising from the awareness of our shared subjection to a condition of absolute vulnerability. An attentiveness to finitude here gains additional weight, because a vivification of our finitude draws from and then helps strengthen a thread of commonality among those who equally share an ultimate fate. This is at the core a *negative* solidarity born of the experience of a common burden, not a positive one arising from the discovery of a common interest among capacious agents in protecting rights. The latter sense is the one to which a liberal nontheist such as Ignatieff would direct us; all human agents can agree that the protection of human rights is crucial to the exercise of our capacities and powers. But this common interest in human rights is, as I have suggested, liable to a continual pressure of disconnection arising from the dispositional bent of the capacious agent with its hegemonic discourse of rights. The problem with this liberal, nontheistic portrait is that while it prefigures well *my* demand for protection, it does not prefigure persuasively what induces me to extend that attentiveness to rights toward those who both lack them and live at substantial geographical or cultural distance from me. When agents are positioned in relatively close geographical and cultural proximity, and we already have a political order in which human rights are relatively secure for most, then a sense of connectedness in the form of an expectation of reciprocity among us can plausibly be imagined as having a reasonable amount of traction. Each of us is seen to be armed to some degree as a rights bearer and has—or at least is relatively close to having—a chair at the common bargaining table. This common self-image of a society like the United States certainly has a good deal of truth in it, but it also can function ideologically to the degree that it encourages a tacit denial of the fact that some sectors of the population remain pretty far from the table. A striking example of this occurred in 2005 in the aftermath of Hurricane Katrina in New Orleans. The mostly black underclass of that city suddenly "appeared" to their more affluent fellow citizens around the country, a phenomenon that made it quite apparent that this category of the population had no real access to the bargaining table.

Clearly such failures of imagination *within* Western democracies are significant. But my emphasis in this chapter is on the even more challenging question of how to project any sense of a bond or connectedness beyond cultural borders and across large geographical spaces onto settings where we have little or no experience of chairs at tables in common. In these venues, those most in need of human rights protection are at a peculiar disadvantage because of the recurrent difficulty capacious agents have in vividly imagining these distant others as being in effective possession of capacities and powers. Moreover, if their efficacy is robustly imagined, the image is always liable to the persistent tendency to interpret that image as hostile and threatening to our identity.

For a capacious self that is susceptible to these sorts of pressures, it is important for it to feel a counterpressure, or resistance, that arises from some experience of distant others as connected through a feeling of common humanity. For the theist, such a bond is made palpable through the belief that we all mutually participate in God's love for his creation. For the nontheist who operates with agency as her only ontological source, the sense of bondedness is figured as forming among possessors of capacities who enjoy the dignity of their self-elevation over the rest of nature.[50] Humanity is constituted by the free joining of capacious hands. For the nontheist who operates with both agency and subjection to mortality as his sources of the self, however, the rudiments of connectedness come to life quite differently. They are vivified through a cultivation of the *experience of* common *subjection,* rather than through a recognition that we *possess* the same *capacities or powers.*[51] An effective sense of common humanity or solidarity seems to me likely to stand a better chance of thriving in the former experiential context than in the latter. In other words, the vivification of a shared constitutive burden has greater promise than does the vivification of a shared possession of powers, when it comes to coaxing my imagination into feeling that most slender, initial bond of commonality across large geographical and cultural distances.[52]

But is this movement of the imagination really just imaginary? A critic of my approach to connectedness has suggested that such a bond is so thin as to have no effect in the real world. And this failure is nowhere more vividly illustrated than in the famous, final scene of Homer's *Iliad*.[53] There Priam, the Trojan king, leaves his besieged city under cover of darkness and makes an unannounced visit to the tent of the Greek leader, Achilles. Both men were in deep mourning: Achilles for his close friend, Patroclus, who had been killed in battle by Priam's son, Hector; and Priam for Hector, whom Achilles killed in retaliation. The visit occurred after Achilles refused to return Hector's body to the Trojans and instead dragged it for several days behind his chariot in a show of ultimate hatred and disrespect. When Priam slipped surreptitiously into Achilles tent, the latter, despite his overpowering rage, did not call the guards to arrest him. Rather he welcomed him and assumed the role of generous host. The meeting generated an extraordinary sharing of grief. But this bond, formed in the vividness of their common subjection to mortality, lasted only a few hours, after which Priam became worried he would be arrested. He then silently slipped out of the tent and returned to Troy.

The critic of my perspective would present this scene as a powerful illustration of just how weak and ephemeral a bond is that arises from nothing more than a shared consciousness of mortality. But I would suggest that at least as strong a case can be made that the moral of Homer's scene is in fact just the reverse. What is stunning about the meeting is the fact that the vivified consciousness of mortality allowed any bond, however slender, to emerge. And that bond was quite significant. It not only allowed the meeting to remain peaceful; it also sustained Achilles' decision to allow Hector's body to be ransomed and returned to Troy for proper funeral rites. It is true that Zeus had earlier instructed Achilles to accept the ransom; and that fact might make one heavily discount the effectiveness of this new bond between the two men. In short, the return of Hector's body was simply forced on Achilles by Zeus. Now that may be partially true, but it also should be remembered that Achilles actually went *further* than Zeus required him to go in responding to Priam. Amazingly, this fierce Greek warrior permitted the Trojan king to prohibit any Greek attacks on the city for several days until the full, public funeral rites had been duly concluded. That space of generosity, that interruption of rage, was created by Achilles, not Zeus.[54]

5

Democracy's Predicament

The last of the five late-modern challenges that face a renewed ethos of citizenship involves the prospects for democracy. Are they bleak or bright, and on what factors should we base our answers? I will argue that democracy faces a predicament. I choose the word *predicament* because it can indicate serious troubles, without necessarily implying completely bleak prospects. In recent years, a variety of political theorists have suggested that democracy is in a condition that is clearly disastrous and where prospects are dismal.[1] I want to resist this thoroughly negative judgment, at least to a degree. The assessment of democracy's condition as disastrous sometimes follows from an overly simple, even romantic conception of democracy. To my mind, a reasonable interpretation of the prospects of democracy needs to start with attentiveness to the complexity of the challenges it faces. I am aware that historically appeals to the complexity of political life have often been made (at least since Burke) in the name of conservative, antidemocratic goals. But that is not necessarily the case. Moreover, whatever dangers might follow from taking complexity too seriously have to be weighed today against the dangers of thinking too simply about democracy.

In Section I, I elucidate three dimensions of our current democratic predicament. Here I should repeat the proviso issued in the Introduction that my analysis is directed primarily at the prosperous Western democracies, especially the United States. The three dimensions are (1) the growth of economic inequality, (2) the changing social bases of the democratic polity, and (3) the fact that the ideal of an autonomous demos has increasingly lost its role as the touchstone of democratic legitimacy. As a way of better locating the character and significance of my response to the democratic predicament, I start in Section II with a consideration of two others' responses. The responses of Sheldon Wolin and Jacques Derrida are shown to have significant flaws, either in their failing to engage the full scope of our late-modern predicament or in their engaging it fully but in an inadequate fashion. On the basis of this critique, I then argue for the reasonableness and comparative superiority of a third response mounted from the perspective of weak ontology and ethos that I have been proposing in the preceding chapters. Finally, in Section III, I take up recurring criticisms that this kind of response is not nearly as convincing as I try to make it. Such concern centers on the suspicion that an approach through a weak ontology and a late-modern ethos ends up being too focused on ethics and not enough on politics. The modes of thought, affective dispositions, and types of action it affirms end up drawing us toward a continual "avoidance" of politics. We need instead a more intransigent, critical orientation, if we are to reinvigorate democratic life.[2]

I. Dimensions of the Predicament

Sheldon Wolin has been one of the most influential political theorists of the last half-century. His many contributions are bookended by the first edition of *Politics and Vision* in 1960 and the second, expanded edition in 2004. I want to take advantage of Wolin's unique perspective on the ideals of modern democracy and on the way he finds them to have been challenged by our current predicament.[3] In this section, I use him to get a purchase on the ontology of modern democracy; and, in the next, I start with a consideration of his response to our current challenge. From his earliest work on, Wolin has deployed a sense of "the political" that is quite useful for getting at the ontological infrastructure of modern democratic life.[4] The central figure of democratic politics for Wolin is that of a continual enactment and expansion of a structure of commonality. Importantly, that structure or logic simultaneously divides the resulting political world into demos, on the one hand, and elites, on the other. In one sense, this ontological figure is not so different from the one that animates Carl Schmitt's picture of the political. Both see politics as a dynamic trajectory through which commonality takes shape and opponents come into sharpened focus. This similarity should not be overemphasized, however. Wolin does not speak the Schmittean language of "friends" and "enemies," a distinction that seems to draw its sustenance from an implicit, pessimistic psychology, for which Schmitt gives no real argument. Wolin speaks, rather, the language of civic contestation, shifting movements, and competing ideas. All this, for Schmitt, would be just so much epiphenomenal "superstructure"; the real determinant of politics will always be the unrelenting antagonism expressed along the single fault line between friends and enemies. Why is Wolin not attracted to this way of categorizing things? I am not aware of his ever having explicitly raised such a question, but I think one can speculate about why Schmitt's scheme would not be taken by Wolin to be satisfactory. One might say that, for Wolin, the "who" of the demos is a dynamic category; when political society is healthy, there is a continual expansion of this "who" and of the issues that knit it together. If you asked Wolin why this process would not stop—as it would for Schmitt— with the solidification of some particular linguistically, culturally, or racially identifiable quality, around which we would then wrap the banner of "friendship," I think he would probably have recourse to something like a universalist notion of human dignity; that is, to some idea that the force of the political is always liable to flame up and expand when we experience, directly or indirectly, material suffering or some form of humiliation at the hands of elites.[5] Democratic politics is ignited when one constituency or another begins to build on commonly shared anger and indignation in a fashion that generates solidarity.

Let me take this Wolinian picture, as I have sketched it so far, as representing a modern conception of the ontology and ethos of a robust democratic life. And let me use that as a background for laying out three dimensions of the democratic predicament pressing on us today. In this background picture, successful democratization is imagined as a kind of self-augmenting force that is continually enhancing the well-being, inclusion, and status of constituencies at the lower reaches of society. Implicit in such a comprehension of democracy is the expectation that the overall distribution of wealth will tend to become more equal over time; or, if not actually becoming more equal in absolute terms, the distribution will nevertheless allow for the continued enhancement of the well-being of the most disadvantaged citizens.[6] But nothing of this sort has been occurring in the United States in recent years. Since the 1970s, there has been a massive explosion in economic inequality.[7] And yet, until relatively recently, this radical assault on the logic of democratic life passed almost unnoticed or was seen as relatively acceptable by large categories of the U.S. population. In short, an unsettling asymmetry seems to have emerged between the clear erosion of democracy and any effective challenge to that erosion arising from a reignition of a strong democratic opposition to it. Here is the first dimension of democracy's late-modern predicament. The democratic spirit seems to be deflating, with relatively little outcry being raised.

The second dimension is at least partially related to the first. It concerns what one might call the changing social bases for the trajectory of democratic commonality. Two phenomena are relevant here. First, there is the way in which a multitude of group identities have come to blur the lines of class identity that, in turn, blurs the basis of democratic solidarity. Groups whose identities cohere around such shared features as language, religion, and ethnicity constitute impediments to progress along a trajectory that demands the continual foregrounding of commonality, not difference. When these forms of identity are strong, it becomes all the more difficult to picture a unified entity we could call the demos that might begin to struggle against the increase in inequality.

An additional change in the social bases of democracy that problematizes the familiar modern portrait of democratic solidarity is growth in the percentage of the population that falls in the middle segment in relation to the distribution of wealth and income. We might visualize this phenomenon (as I suggested in the Introduction) by abandoning the traditional image of wealth distribution in Western democracies as being pyramid-shaped and beginning to represent it as more diamond-shaped. The bottom of the diamond would not be a perfect point, because that would imply that only a miniscule number of people are in the poorest position. Rather, we would imagine the bottom of the diamond being filed off somewhat.[8] Using this image, we can further distinguish between the more inegalitarian Western democracies, such as the United States, and the less inegalitarian ones, such as Sweden or Germany.[9] The former would be taller diamonds with bottoms that are filed off rather far, whereas the latter would be shorter diamonds with bottoms that are filed off to a lesser degree. For my purposes, the diamond shape, with its broadest category in the middle, is useful in drawing our attention to the reality that the great majority that might constitute the classic subject of democratic will-formation cannot be composed exclusively of a category that is both poorest and numerically the largest. This is so, for the simple reason that there is no such category.

My emphasis on the middle segment might appear to be the start of a celebratory argument for such a society's having become a successful democracy in the sense that more people are relatively well-off. But there is little reason to celebrate, given that in some Western democracies, especially the United States, the large middle segment of the population coexists with a continuing growth in inequality, as well as the continued existence of a substantial "underclass" of impoverished citizens.[10] My point in calling attention to this combination of characteristics is to emphasize that the success of efforts to reduce that inequality and poverty will likely have to depend on creative ways of imagining coalitions between poorest and elements of the middle segment of the population.

As a rough generalization about this middle, I would describe the population in it as being relatively removed from real material misery.[11] This does not mean that everyone in this middle category is economically comfortable. Many toward the bottom of this segment face recurring economic insecurity (especially in the United States, with its lack of a national system of health care). They may, for example, face dislocations such as layoffs that come with their jobs being shifted to less economically developed countries. And the replacement jobs they find are often ones that pay less. A problem that this segment of society poses for enhancing democracy is that its members see themselves as enjoying relative economic success, even if that success always remains somewhat uncertain. And, especially in the United States, they also often prove to be relatively deaf to strong democratic appeals, on the one hand, and quite receptive to appeals that play on sentiments of resentment toward those who are culturally or racially "different" or below them economically, on the other.[12] Such a population category is deeply problematic for any political program that envisions the future in terms of a simple reignition of the classic logic of modern democratic solidarity.

If the second dimension of the late-modern predicament renders the social basis of democratic commonality problematic, the third dimension renders a comparable effect in relation to the normative core of the modern *ideal* of robust democracy. The issue here is that the simple, powerful image of a self-governing demos is no longer appropriate as the primary telos of democratic solidarity. I mean here that we can no longer legitimately appeal to a figure of collective autonomy; that is, to a macrosubject governing itself sovereignly. Rousseau was perhaps the greatest proponent of this grand figure of democratic normativity in modern Western political thought. Such a collective subject is, however, increasingly seen today as too prone to mask coercion with soothing democratic imagery. Of course, many modern liberals have always been deeply skeptical of any talk of the self-governing demos; but this figure has continued to engage the imagination of radical democrats and democratic socialists since the eighteenth century. Now, however, the number of thinkers who would explicitly defend it is declining, even if some of them continue to allow it to operate implicitly in their reflections. Whether explicit or implicit, the continued attachment to the core notion of a latent, collective subject that can emerge finally as the ruling force of society—the sovereign demos—feeds illusory hopes. One of those hopes is that the problems of the rich Western democracies admit of simple solutions.

A prominent example of the move away from the idea of a collective macro-subject of democracy is Jürgen Habermas. In his later work, we see a renunciation of the ideal of a collective democratic subject. In *Between Facts and Norms,* Habermas argues that we must give up the dangerous figure of "a goal-oriented subject writ large."[13] Also, from a more clearly Marxist direction, there has been a comparable renunciation of the ideal of an all-inclusive, collective revolutionary subject that would eventually govern in a purely democratic fashion. Ernesto Laclau, embracing the late-modern insight regarding the constitutive relationship of identity and difference, has developed a notion of politics in which a democratically organized movement or regime must never be comprehended as the embodiment of some pure democratic will but rather always as an instance of the "hegemony" of some "populist" coalition over its rivals.[14] The normative value of this new formulation is that political coercion is less likely to be masked by the claim that its exercise in the name of the demos automatically establishes its legitimacy.

Wolin appears to share this growing skepticism about collective autonomy. Over his career, he has become increasingly worried about attributing any emphatically positive characteristics to the governing will of large, national states. Such a will is simply too likely to use its claim to embody a universally valid form of democratic autonomy to disguise imperialism abroad and repression of its opponents at home.[15] But Wolin also provides an example of the tendency I just noted among some democratic theorists to combine an explicit distrust of collective autonomy with an implicit appeal to the aesthetic-expressive force of the ideal of a potentially emergent demos. This combination makes it all the more difficult, as I will show in the next section, to think anew about how we should imagine the normative core of late-modern democracy.

II. Late-Modern Responses

I turn now to consider some attempts to respond to the democratic predicament I have delineated. More particularly, I am interested in efforts that seek in some way to rethink or revivify the onto-logic and ethos of democracy, and thereby contribute to a reconceptualization of the normative core of democratic life.

Again, it is useful initially to turn to Wolin, because he not only gives us a general sense of what modern democracy has meant but also of what its current prospects are. Our "postmodern" condition, he asserts, is such that the future looks extremely bleak. The structures of the national state in the United States and of global capitalism stifle any real hope for renewing democracy. Accordingly, in regard to the first dimension of our predicament—growing inequality and disempowerment of citizens—Wolin seems to find no really effective way forward, at least not at the national level. Also, the oppressiveness of large political and economic structures is further enhanced by one aspect of the second dimension of the late-modern predicament; namely, the one posed by the growing prominence of all kinds of identity claims. Wolin sees these pretty much as a curse on democratic life, arguing that their emphasis on differences in identity is deeply harmful to any attempt to move along the trajectory of democratic commonality.[16]

If Wolin persistently worries about how contemporary politics has been too engaged with issues of identity recognition, he totally ignores the other changed social basis of democratic life; namely, the existence of a large middle segment that has something more to lose than its "chains." Wolin writes as if rich democracies had a distribution of wealth and income that could be adequately represented by the figure of a pyramid. On this view, the demos is imagined as constituting itself from the lowest and most numerous segment. Here we begin to see Wolin aligning an empirical view of the social bases of contemporary society with tacit ontological and normative commitments. The resulting, almost mythical, image of the demos emerges only occasionally into full view, as when he asserts that democracy is "an elemental politics about the needs and aspirations of the Many" (Wolin's capitalization).[17] This image, I would suggest, is a central, if usually implicit, animating figure in Wolin's democratic theory.

What the figure offers us is, however, problematic in both an empirical and normative sense. Empirically, the notion of a potential, radical majority formed from the great base of the social pyramid—all those who must "scratch out a decent existence," as Wolin puts it—simply does not correspond to reality in societies like the United States, where the distribution of wealth has more the shape of a diamond.[18] Wolin's failure to acknowledge this reality allows him to make some strong claims about contemporary democracy that appear to be far more questionable when one thinks in terms of its diamond shape. Most important, he contends that the *absence* of a powerful, radical democratic movement today can only be attributed to one thing: the overwhelmingly repressive effects of the structures of state and capitalist power.[19] If his picture of extreme oppression is wrong, however, that would make the condition of democracy less dire and its predicament more complex than he thinks.

It is now not difficult to determine where Wolin leaves us in regard to my third dimension of the democratic predicament; namely, the growing illegitimacy of appeals to the ideal of a self-governing demos. His apparently explicit rejection of that ideal is undermined by his tacit appeal to the absent presence of "the Many." One sees this in the fact that his increasingly pessimistic judgments about the prospects for democracy are deeply colored by a feeling of mourning that arises from a sense of our having squandered the possibility of achieving authentic rule by the demos. Today, he concludes, we are left with only minimal and occasional relief from this regrettable fate. All that we can see on the immediate horizon are specific opportunities for "combining traditional localism with postmodern centrifugalism." Wolin speaks here of "fugitive democracy," a term meant to emphasize evasive and episodic qualities that keep opposition mobile enough to escape temporarily from the crushing oppression of the state and capitalism.[20]

Now the idea of taking democracy to be, at least partially, an evasive, local, and mobile—fugitive—assemblage of movements rather than just "a possible constitutional form for an entire society," is a good one.[21] But the air of pessimism that pervades its introduction implicitly trades on an imagined loss of some grander possibility; namely, one in which the "Many" exert their will. Such an image and mood seem to me to imbue democratic thought and action with an unnecessary gloom as to their real value and prospects. The imagined loss of a grander possibility has two strong—but resistible to my mind—effects in the way we view the political. First, it burns into our reflections an almost overwhelming sense of the oppressiveness of the structures of capitalism and liberal democratic institutions. Against this, it seems to me that we do better to look for palpable criteria of greater or lesser oppressiveness that might guide the development of a graduated repertoire of democratic practices. The second effect of the imagined loss of a grander possibility is that potential allies in democratic movements may be encouraged to view one another more easily with resentment. I mean here that a democratic actor whose anger and indignation might draw continual fuel from the Wolinian sense of a vision betrayed is likely to jump to quick conclusions regarding a potential ally's failure to see its way quickly onto the proffered democratic trajectory. That group, in short, is likely to be sized up as either ill-willed or thickheaded, or both.

If one turns from Wolin to another well-known response to the late-modern predicament, one also finds an emphasis on something like his notion of "fugitive" democracy. This is apparent in Jacques Derrida's later thinking about the prospects for robust democratic life. Writing in the wake of the end of the Cold War in the early 1990s, Derrida sees political order as always "haunted" by the tragedies, missed radical opportunities, horrible injustices of the past, as well as by the possible demands of future others. This haunting holds open the possibility of "another concept of the political" and animates the idea of a "democracy-to-come."[22]

Like Wolin's, Derrida's judgment of Western democracy's current state is deeply negative. Our prospects for things such as decreasing the degree of inequality and disempowerment, he writes, are "bleak, . . . almost black."[23] Against that sort of background, glimpses of democratic hope are indeed fugitive. Despite this initial similarity between the two thinkers, Derrida's sense of fugitivity possesses a distinctive difference from Wolin's; and this difference gives Derrida's response to the late-modern challenges to democracy a significant advantage.

In Wolin, the concept of fugitivity is given life primarily on the basis of his judgment regarding the dismal fate of politics today. This makes his ethos of the fugitive cohere around the quality of escape or flight from domination by the existing economic and political structures. But what would happen to fugitivity if Wolin were wrong in this thoroughly bleak assessment of our political fate? If prospects now are indeed better than he thinks, or if they come to be so in the future, then our emphasis on the value of comprehending social relations through the category of the fugitive would, accordingly, lose its rationale. The issue here is simply that the source of the positive valuation of fugitivity for Wolin is primarily a strategic judgment based on an empirical assessment of the bleakness of political circumstances.

Derrida's valuation of the fugitive as a response to the late-modern democratic predicament is partially based on such a judgment, but it is deeply dependent on something else as well. Fugitivity has an ontological source along with a political one. The difference this makes is that it allows for moderating the bleakness of one's political judgment without that having the effect of abandoning the value of fugitivity. This is no small advantage.

Like Wolin and Derrida, many on the political left today have developed a propensity for issuing pretty sweeping judgments about the bleakness or darkness of our times. There are, no doubt, some real grounds for such worries. But it might be advisable to keep a somewhat stronger sense of historical comparison in front of us regarding such judgments, so that we might have a basis for progressively shading our determinations of light and darkness. For example, when I think of truly dark times, I think of how Walter Benjamin must have felt in September 1940 as he fled the Nazi war machine, attempting to escape across the border from France to Spain. The horrendous fate of Jews was becoming clearer every day; fascism's grip on Europe seemed to tighten more each month; and the world was mired in the worst economic depression the twentieth century had witnessed. That was darkness. By comparison, I have to see the first decade of the twenty-first century as markedly better in its prospects for democracy. Not good, perhaps, but better.

My point here is that Derrida might have been persuaded to see the political world as less bleak, but that would not have crucially impaired his affirmation of fugitivity as an essential motif in a late-modern ethos of democratic life. As I said, the emphasis on this value emerges from his ontology of difference, his sense that the world is a continual play of presence and absence.[24] For someone with such a view, any attempt to see being as a kind of fixed presence of some sort is misguided and only fuels our conception of ourselves as grandly capacious in all matters conceptual and practical. It is against this modern propensity that the main significance of fugitivity becomes apparent for Derrida (and me). The particular connotations of fugitivity that one now emphasizes shift slightly but importantly from those Wolin highlights. Less emphasis now falls on being in "flight from" and more on the episodic, the decentered, the singular in character, and the difficult-to-grasp. One is attentive to such features of the world, because to highlight them is to reaffirm continually an ontology of presencing or becoming, a being that exceeds our categories and structures.[25] And to be attentive in this way is to begin to prefigure the virtue of presumptive generosity as central to a democratic ethos.

The theme of generosity to, or hospitality for, the radically "other" is a consistent theme in Derrida. But he tended to be more interested in the ethical core of this theme (following Levinas) than in its political implications. In *Specters* and other later works, he did begin to attend more to the latter, referring to the need to allow ourselves to be haunted by, and obligated to, the idea of a "democracy-to-come."[26] But this idea remains quite abstract, in the sense that although I, as a democratic citizen, have this intense obligation, what exactly it might mean to engage political life in the here-and-now remains more fugitive than one might wish.[27]

Let me use this issue as the point of entry into a final response to the predicament of late-modern democracy; namely, the perspective I have been trying to develop in conversation with Connolly. In earlier chapters, I touched on Connolly's interpretation of presumptive generosity in relation to the challenge of identity politics. He speaks of the importance of "critical responsiveness" to the phenomenon of natality in political life; that is, to the continual emergence of new identities as well as the way in which they tend to provoke discomfort, resentment, and hostility from established constituencies. The cultivation of critical responsiveness involves attempting to dampen the propensity to react negatively to the "politics of enactment" and to give novel political movements some space in which to bring to public life some of their particular identity and its concerns.[28] It could also be turned toward exploring the possibility of new openings toward existing constituencies that are familiar objects of hostility.

What is distinctive about critical responsiveness, as opposed, say, to Derrida's hospitality, is that the former is at one end of a range of dispositions constituting "agonistic respect" that Connolly finds appropriate in late-modern politics at different times and with different movements. In short, critical responsiveness is an *initial* disposition that may be legitimately deemphasized as a new claim or movement gains ground in political space. In its place, other dispositions, both positive and negative, become more appropriate. The most negative would be outright violent conflict, if the movement really threatened, for example, the fundamental values of democracy; or political opposition, if the movement proved to be in favor of political goals that were ultimately found to be unjust. Alternatively, if the movement were to remain mildly but persistently offensive in some way, one might cultivate an attitude of "studied indifference," whereby one would attempt to avoid festering resentment toward the group in question, while having as little as possible to do with it.[29]

More positively, one might find dimensions of commonality existing between this group and one's own, and thus that a "selective collaboration" with it in political action makes sense.[30] Connolly does not say a great deal about what is involved here, but he makes it clear that this engagement and potential for coalition is best imagined with the aid of Giles Deleuze's metaphor of a "rhizome."[31] In contrast with the more traditional tree metaphor, according to which a central, common trunk (of values and identity) nourishes and supports all the many branches (groups), rhizomes are types of plants that have no trunk but rather throw out roots and shoots in multiple directions. This late-modern image illustrates a radically different way of thinking about the commonality that is displayed in political relationships as compared to the modern image of a single, broad trajectory of commonality that brings the demos to life. In sum, rhizomatic democratic theorists do not dream of the emergent demos but rather of fluctuating and transient *demoi* (the plural of *demos*).

In referring to "selective collaboration," Connolly clearly is thematizing a politics of coalition building among constituencies that may share some interests but not others. As one tries to imagine this trajectory of the political, one can also see how an initial disposition of presumptive generosity becomes relevant in an additional way. Going beyond Connolly in a significant direction, Rom Coles usefully suggests how valuable such generosity can be in the *internal* workings of coalition building, as opposed to its value as one initially reacts to the appearance of some novel political movement. The building of coalitions under the challenges of late modernity means that democratic political ties are harder to weave together and maintain than, for example, when a fifth-century Athenian politician was trying to draw the demos together on, say, the issue of going to war. The harder it is to craft commonality, the more crucial it is to cultivate a disposition that *both* confronts frustration, irritation, and disappointment (with those with whom one would coalesce) *and* "keeps one coming back for more."[32]

Clearly, a rhizomelike image of democratic coalition within diamond-shaped societies can only gain traction if all dreams—especially ones whose attraction continues even after explicit disavowal of their content—of a sovereign demos have been relinquished. Wolin, as I indicated before, seems to have boxed himself into a corner, where his sketch of repressive economic and political structures is so totalized that one almost cannot help generating simultaneously an implicit political vision that holds emancipation to be something achievable only in some sort of collective transcendence of such structures. But social structures are not like hard-walled boxes that contain soft subjects; rather they must constantly be reproduced by the actions of subjects. My whole effort in articulating an ethos of democratic citizenship takes shape around the idea that it makes a difference how we go about "living the . . . structures that the contemporary age makes mandatory," more particularly the modern, bureaucratic state and market economy.[33] Here the rhizome image is again helpful. As gardeners know only too well, rhizomes such as bamboo do not knock structures (fences, borders) down; rather they grow around, into, and under them, thereby slowly, but markedly, changing the character of the landscape. Such an image can be understood to include a wide range of initiatives that seek to achieve substantial democratic goals. Thus it is not hard to envision coalitions being drawn together that have the potential to begin undermining the high degree of inequality in the United States. This change would not occur in one grand program but rather piecemeal, over time. Looking forward, it does not seem unrealistic to imagine some form of universal health care being adopted in the United States; the same could be said regarding changes in the tax code that would begin to reverse the trend toward ever greater concentrations of wealth. Such changes could measurably have an impact on the unfairness and unmet needs one finds on the lower levels of society. Will these changes actually occur? Perhaps not; my aim, however, is not to predict but rather only suggest that it does not take a demos in the classical sense to slide such matters onto a plausible political agenda.

At this point, a critic might respond by pressing the bottom-line question: Would the change I just sketched *really* constitute a demolition of *the structure* of inequality? From the perspective I am advocating, this question has a kind of unreal quality to it, rather like the question: When is *the demos* finally going to become the ruling force in society?

Let me turn now to how the present response comes to terms with that aspect of the second late-modern dimension of predicament that I called the phenomenon of the large middle segment of the population in rich, Western democracies. This category is peculiarly situated. On the one hand, many within it are relatively well off materially and culturally; thus their interests overlap partially with those of the more directly hegemonic interests in these societies. On the other hand, people in the middle periodically face substantial threats to their sense of cultural identity and economic well-being. That undertone of insecurity is important to the way I want to identify this segment. Uncertainty and anxiety often engender citizens who are subtly primed to react to political phenomena with resentment and low-grade hostility. In a world characterized—at both the intrastate and global levels—by rapid changes associated with globalization (such as outsourcing), by the dialectic of what Connolly calls "pluralization and fundamentalization," and by the continual chorus of claims associated with identity politics, it is of real significance to democratic political life that citizens in this segment be disposed to manifest an ethos of agonistic respect whose first gesture to the oncoming phenomena of public life is presumptive generosity.[34]

Exactly who should be counted as falling within this middle segment in a given Western society varies from country to country. In one sense, this category includes all those who are not suffering real material deprivation (food, shelter, basic health), even if they periodically face substantial threats to their sense of economic security. But such a purely economic criterion is too inclusive; it fails to take into account those who are separated from the typical member of the middle section because of race, minority nationality or religion, or some other cultural marker. For these groups, it does not make sense to argue that presumptive generosity should have the same sort of initial primacy. Such groups do not occupy a cultural center from whose perspective resentment is generated toward symbolic threats or disturbances from the margins of society. Of course, I am not claiming that groups such as African Americans in the United States don't manifest resentment in politics but only that their resentment is more heavily rooted in historical experiences with oppression and thus in a legitimate, sense-of-justice-driven reaction to the continuing weight of real oppression.

I want to shift the focus of discussion now to how a late-modern ethos responds to the problem of growing inequality. This response does not take the form of a systematic argument demonstrating the illegitimacy of high levels of inequality; rather it emphasizes something about the figure of human being that slightly, but significantly, shifts the background assumptions we carry with us as we perceive and dispute matters in morals and politics.[35] In Chapters 3 and 4, I have assembled the components of a distinctive way of thinking about human dignity. This involves, first, a particular way of interpreting our unique status as creatures that seek and make meaning. We make and remake meaning through our capacity for language; and we always continue uncertainly along this path, because our ontological sources are never capable of being fully articulated. And we seek meaning because of consciousness of our finitude. In Chapter 4, I fleshed out further the character of this consciousness of our subjection to this condition, as well as the way it offers us a figuration that deflates illusions of capaciousness and sovereignty that have adhered to traditional liberal notions of dignity. This figure of the human does not, moreover, depend on a theological source for authoritative limits on our capaciousness. Such limits come rather from our facing the full character of our intransigent inarticulacy and mortality. It is the common subjection to this condition that provides us with a weak ontological illumination of human equality. Our common lot, our common vulnerability as mortals, is the basis on which we begin to imagine the solidarity of humanity.

I would argue that the effect of embracing the figure of dignity just sketched would be to dispose us skeptically toward the sort of increases in inequality that have emerged in recent years. What I mean might be illuminated by an analogy from the law. Lawyers speak of a certain category of cases where one party bears "the burden of proof" in relation to the other. My suggestion is that a democratic ethos animated by a sense of human dignity such as I have laid out would be one in which the burden of proof for a citizen would fall more "naturally" and heavily on those who support a status quo tolerant of massive inequality than is the case at present.

This shifting of the burden would be elicited by the following sorts of considerations. In my reconfigured portrait of dignity, the deepest sense of equality now comes from a common vulnerability, the shared knowledge of our mortality. Now in one sense, this kind of vulnerability might be seen to imply that high levels of economic inequality would be perfectly acceptable: Because we all will die, why should having more or less wealth matter at all? But ever since the ancient Greeks thought about the free shaping of public meaning, people have realized that the good life is negatively influenced by material deprivation. The seeking and making of meaning flourishes to a greater degree when my life is not dominated by the activity of staving off serious deprivation. A life so consumed is an affront to human dignity. Thus the massive growth in economic inequality in a society such as that of the United States, with some being left seriously disadvantaged and others living a life filled with an incredible surplus of goods, seems deeply at odds with the sort of ethos that is congruent with the orientation I have been sketching. If so, then our sense of justice would be drawn toward distributions of wealth that would eliminate serious deprivation.

The preceding orientation of judgment remains *passive* in a significant sense. It is essentially a judgment about distributions or outcomes, not about *active* participation toward the achievement of such effects. Is there anything in my late-modern ethos that might dispose a citizen to value more rather than less participation in public life? I would say yes, but the disposition involved is fairly minimal. If dignity is understood in terms of meaning-seeking and meaning-making, as I have defined it, and we realize that such processes are always incomplete because of the limits of articulacy, then we have (as I suggested in earlier chapters) sketched ourselves as creatures on a journey whose goal is always being discovered/created. And this goal will always be partially shared and partially contested by others; agonism and plurality are part of our world. If I understand myself in these terms, there will be a subtle, but perhaps not insignificant, gravitational pull toward more rather than less participation in public life. If we think here of a spectrum of types of lives distinguished in terms of the degree to which activity is more or less bound up in the definition of the actor, we might put the Aristotelian individual on one end, and the individual imagined by economists and their allies in political science on the other. Flourishing for the former is dependent on taking action in public life; flourishing for the latter can be achieved when an individual is not required to take any action at all, because action counts as a "cost" to be avoided. Human being, as I have sketched it, sits far closer to the Aristotelian figure than to the economically rational one.[36]

One remaining aspect of inequality stands at some distance from the foregoing discussion but is, nevertheless, important. This aspect involves the issue of inequality across species. I touched on this matter briefly in Chapter 3. It concerns how Connolly, as well as many other thinkers one might identify as poststructuralists or postmodernists, seem quite comfortable with the idea of toppling humans from their traditional preeminence in the order of being, which they have enjoyed in Western civilization since antiquity, and which modernity certainly did nothing to challenge. In this matter, as in so many others, the toppling maneuver works by exposing how binaries such as human/nonhuman express not naturally given fault lines in being but rather human constructions that are often also carriers of power or domination. Such exposure works so as to erase lines that were previously sharp.

But after blurring the human/nonhuman line, how does one go about redrawing it in some way that allows us to avoid affirming the sort of disturbing choices that traditional political theorists would argue we are likely to make unless we affirm a bright and clear line? I am referring here to choices like the one I mentioned in Chapter 3: preferring the preservation of a rare species of bird to the prevention of genocide. Connolly clearly wants to be able to prefer the prevention of genocide, while nevertheless still partially erasing the line. In support of the latter, he and others can legitimately point to ongoing research that continually discovers new facts about animals, relating to their toolmaking, social coordination, learning capacity, and emotional life.[37] Most recently, he has expressed the view that perhaps we can allow humans some "priority," but it must be a "modest" one. Perhaps, Connolly concludes, we should imagine ourselves as "shepherds of being, more than masters of the rest of nature."[38]

I like this way of putting the matter. The crucial question then becomes one of whether or not my reinterpretation of dignity, fleshed out in Chapters 3 and 4, supports a view of human priority or elevation that is sufficiently modest. My claim to sufficiency rests on two of the features that I have argued are constitutive of human dignity; more specifically, on the ways in which these features deflate and decenter the traditional modern figure of dignity revolving around the sovereign capacities of reason and freedom. The first refiguration expresses how human meaning-making involves not just our unique capacity for ordinary language communication but also, along with that, a unique *in-capacity*: our constitutive inarticulacy. For such a being, any conduct that understands itself as a manifestation of our character as free and rational sovereign masters of being will appear as a distortion or forgetting of our peculiar, limited capaciousness. Second, my interpretation of dignity also builds into it a sense of ourselves as mortal creatures. Here again, conduct that would be sovereign betrays a kind of imbalance or lack of truthfulness about our character. In sum, I would contend that this refigured portrait of dignity has more affiliation with the vocation of shepherd than of master.

III. Objections

I want to turn now to objections that have been directed at the idea of a late-modern ethos of democracy. The most significant ones suggest that such an ethos fails adequately to confront undemocratic movements and arrangements of power or to inspire democratic renewal. It gives us what is, in effect, a "politics of avoidance" that is deleterious to the future of democracy.[39] This criticism can be divided into two related lines of argument. First, there is concern that the central ideas of weak ontology and the ethos it animates lead us finally to nothing more than a paralyzing tentativeness and uncertainty in political engagement, mixed with a simple and inappropriate generosity toward the enemies of democracy. What we need as strong democrats today is more decisiveness and less generosity (A). Second, this specific blunting of the critical edge of democratic theory is really part of a larger conceptual operation that domesticates and imprisons democratic impulses. The gist of this fatal maneuver is captured by my use of Taylor's phrase "living the structures" of the modern state and market economy. The acceptance of this constrained form of life depletes a democratic imagination that should be animated rather by images of bursting through such structures (B).

A. Avoiding Politics

What sort of orientation to politics are we really given by the idea of a late-modern ethos animated by a contestable, weak ontology and sustaining a presumptive generosity? It is, critics argue, one largely eaten up by uncertainty and tentativeness, and when it does finally issue in some engagement with politics, that orientation is the decidedly inappropriate one of being generous. Both of these orientations are deeply inappropriate for democratic citizens today whose primary stance should be one of "conviction, condemnation, and denunciation . . ."[40]

Let me turn first to the charge that weak ontology leads to a tentativeness and uncertainty that makes the democratic citizen weak-kneed. Because his beliefs are rooted in a weak ontology, whose fundamentals cannot claim to possess absolute truth, all the beliefs animated by that ontology will be embraced in a tentative way. One cannot have adequate motivation to engage fully in the agonistic contests of politics on the basis of such "weak affirmation."[41] Richard Flathman has likened my citizen to his dog who, when the door is opened each morning to let him go outside, seems not to be able to decide whether to leave the house or stay inside.[42] He sniffs the air, makes false starts, and looks around anxiously, but he cannot bring himself to get past the threshold. Because I had a cat with the same tendencies, I know this can be a real problem, at least in the world of pets. But I see no reason to accept this characterization of indecision as at all descriptive of a citizen who affirms a late-modern ethos. Flathman contrasts my citizen with the one he favors who is motivated by William James's strong "will to believe."[43] James's position is spelled out in his fascinating 1897 essay, "The Will to Believe."[44] My problem with Flathman lies not in his affirmation of James's arguments but rather with his equation of my position with the one James was targeting in that essay. He was trying to refute what was at that time seen by many to be a thoroughly modern, scientific stance regarding the proper grounds for belief: one should simply refuse to believe anything or act on it until the relevant hypothesis was supported by sufficient evidence. What James pointed out was that in our most basic commitments, that is, our existential or religious beliefs and actions, we cannot typically expect to have such evidence in hand before the need for judgment is pressed on us. In some cases, we may find that evidence bearing directly on the judgment does eventually appear; in others, no evidence may ever fully determine or change our beliefs. In this area of basic commitments, then, we end up making judgments that just seem somehow to best "fit" us and to be capable of continually drawing out our best efforts.

If one attends carefully to the claims I have been making about a weak ontology and its animation of a particular ethos, the ironic conclusion is that my position is far closer to James's—and thus Flathman's—than to that of his opponents. This should become clearer, if we return to the distinction I made in Chapter 2 between commitment and conviction. In my Taylorian account of sources, something is wrong with claims about absolute conviction as to the truth of my interpretation of some core ontological figure. The problem of final inarticulacy always confounds such claims when they refer to the figures that provide us with the most basic orientation for our lives. But the recognition that absolute *cognitive conviction* about such things is something of a category mistake can be joined perfectly reasonably with the *deepest commitment* to my sources and the actions I find to offer the best expression of that commitment in a given set of circumstances. I see no problem of havering or lack of motivation or fortitude in this way of tending to the world.

If my democratic citizen might thus be absolved of a terminal tentativeness, what about her cultivation of the virtue of presumptive generosity? Is it really as hopelessly naive and idealistic as critics such as Jodi Dean make it out to be; and does its cultivation also draw attention away from real dangers in political life?[45] One can begin to get some purchase on this question by comparing her charge against presumptive generosity with the kind of charge often made of those who—typically on religious grounds—advocate nonviolence in all dangerous political or military situations. Critics will perhaps admire such a person's pacifist motivations and even the effects of his actions in some situations, but they will find him woefully naive in his beliefs about the adequacy of his strategy as a response to the full horrors that politics and war bring our way. For example, how would Gandhi and his movement have fared if they had faced the Nazis rather than the British? Dean lambastes the idea of presumptive generosity as similarly guileless.

If Dean's portrayal of a late-modern ethos were accurate, her criticism might also be apt. But, as we saw earlier, presumptive generosity is not a one-size-fits-all political response. It is intended as an initial response designed to restrain the resentment and hostility we otherwise tend to bring into public engagement, especially when our opponents are part of a marginal group or make unfamiliar claims that disturb our settled sense of identity. Although neither Connolly nor I have elaborated at great length on succeeding, alternative responses, it is eminently clear that presumptive generosity is not intended as an exclusive mode of political engagement.

Dean's thorough condemnation of presumptive generosity thus simply misfires from the start.

B. Depleting the Democratic Imagination

But if Dean's specific criticism is off target, perhaps it contains a more legitimate concern that can be stated in a more powerful way as a claim about the regrettable effects of what some have called the recent "ethical turn" in political theory.[46] This new emphasis can be described in different ways, but however it is characterized, the critics find its manifestations to be merely variants of the dangerous disease of apoliticalness. It is especially insidious, Dean contends, when it emerges from quarters (such as mine, Connolly's, or Judith Butler's) that have previously been associated with some sort of critical, political theory. For example, referring to my own earlier work on the Frankfurt School of critical theory, Dean says that my new thinking about ethos regrettably trades in the classical "immanent critique" of society for a politically pusillanimous one absorbed with the "immanent affirmation" of all political movements and values, regardless of how heinous they may be. When this undiscriminating affirmation is joined with a stress on the cultivation of the actor's dispositions, we end up with something like a twenty-first century version of Hegel's "beautiful soul," the difference being that this model preserves itself from the ugliness of the real world not by remaining within the inner citadel of the pure conscience, but rather by pantheistically assuming all otherness in the world is primarily infused with beauty. Thus Dean's final judgment: "What a beautiful notion. What a nice, nice approach."[47]

And it is precisely the wrong approach for the dark times in which we live. According to Dean, we do not need to hear homilies about "living the structures" of the modern state and market economy, but rather directions for smashing and transcending those structures. Our enemies are self-evident: "the religious, nationalist and market fundamentalisms dominating contemporary social and political life."[48] Our response should be just as self-evident. We need to renounce the distractions of "vulgar culturalism," as Antonio Arroyo calls it, and place ourselves firmly on the path of radical democratic solidarity.[49]

We are told that we have clear choices in very dark times. But weren't we exhorted in an uncomfortably similar way by President Bush in 2001, when he intoned: "You are either with us or against us" in the war against terrorism?[50] Are you friend or enemy? My reaction to such loaded choices in both the case of terrorism and the democratic predicament is to refuse to be volunteered for either option. The recourse to such rhetorical strategies is an invitation to distort and oversimplify the hard work of political reflection and action.

For Dean, the idea of living economic and political structures in a critical way constitutes a "deadly assumption."[51] We need to think instead in terms of radically new social structures. But what exactly that means remains at the level of the vaguest possible suggestion. All we are really left with is the imputation that "living the structures" amounts to living as a domesticated animal without any "critical . . . oppositional edge" that can be used to bust through the walls of our cages.[52]

The notion of a critical edge or standpoint is a crucial one. But the idea that the promise that such a standpoint can only be brought to life by a sweeping vision of the demos, animating radically new political and economic structures, has not always fared well in the past. Insofar as Dean's claims about structures tacitly depend on holding out such a promise, there is reason to be skeptical.

But perhaps we can construe the force of her claims . . . well . . . more generously; that is, in a way that is harder for my late-modern ethos to refute. What if Dean were to forgo the implication of transcending structures and simply argue instead that a late-modern ethos is incapable of prefiguring at all a normative difference between compliant and contestatory reactions to the structures one is living. The arguments I have made so far might be seen as flawed in that they do not distinguish an ontological figure that thematizes democratic contestation in a way that draws attention to a critical standpoint, from whose perspective we can pick out clearly illegitimate assaults on the dignity of common people. My perspective seems only to recognize failures to be presumptively generous, a virtue that gets its ultimate sense from the idea of witnessing or mimicking the ontological figure of presencing. But what gives sense to the decision to contest something as illegitimate in politics? Those who have affirmed an ontology of presencing or becoming, drawing from Nietzsche and Heidegger, have typically defined such becoming as agonistic. Might that agonistic dimension not prefigure the ubiquity of political contestation? It could indeed. There is a problem, however. The simple figure of agonism seems to underwrite an affirmation of any and all political contestation. If that is so, is there really any basis on which to think about a more legitimate agonism versus less legitimate, more violence-prone forms?

The figure needed would be one that draws our attention toward some sense of the normative bonds of intersubjectivity. Think, for example, of Levinas's ontological scene of the self confronted by the face of the other and the unlimited obligation it posits for the self.[53] This figuration has certainly been immensely influential for the way Derrida thinks about ethics and politics. It gives him the basis for thinking of the ethical-political as involved with a working back and forth between an unconditional demand for hospitality or justice and its relation of tension with the concrete, limited rights and obligations associated with specific laws that apply, for example, to refugees or asylum seekers.[54] Is there anything in the weak ontology I have outlined that plays a structurally similar role in a late-modern ethos?

So far, there is not; and there should be. What is needed can best be figured by elaborating further the sense of ordinary language communication and drawing on the understanding of human dignity developed in Chapter 4. I have thematized this process largely in terms of the self and its meaning-making and meaning–seeking in relation to sources of the self. But I have not really focused upon the self's reproduction of prevailing social norms in this process; that is, the way in which ongoing communicative interaction sustains and yet, at times, contests existing normative structures. If this is what is needed, then Levinas's figure of the self and the face of the other will not be much help. This is because, for him, ordinary language is not a primordial part of that scene; the face just somehow transmits to me the absolute ethical obligation I have to the other. This obligation somehow exists before that which is public and normative.

Another familiar, orienting ontological scene comes from Louis Althusser. This is the famous scene of "interpellation," in which the self responds to a call from the other. This other is a policeman who calls, "You there!" And the self that turns in response is thereby interpellated into existence as a subject of power, a subject who is accountable in normative terms that are not its own.[55] This figure has been modulated in various ways. Judith Butler, for example, has modified it so that the self is continually enacting its gender as it performs the scripts that social authorities call for and expect; and, in so doing, it invests what is conventional—gender—with the status of a strong

ontology. In *Gender Trouble,* power is thus more primordial that either ontology or ethics; and, as a consequence, we must contest ontological scripts
in order to modify power relations.[56]

My point in drawing attention to such philosophical contributions is to
suggest that we are accumulating a rich set of possible ontological scenes
that can provide a vivid portrayal of the basic conceptualizations of our
sources; and this, in turn, helps prefigure more specific moral-political perceptions and judgments about self, other, power, and the force of norms.
But I have also left one such scene off of my list; and this oversight is quite
common. The scene is one that we get from Habermas. It is not, however,
the one that typically comes to mind when scholars think of his work. That
scene is, of course, the famous (or infamous) "ideal speech situation," in
which actors, motivated only by reason, are arrayed in front of one another
and exchange arguments until consensus is reached.[57] Less familiar is a
scene that is just as basic conceptually as this one. The former scene is part
of the explication Habermas gives of the most fundamental concept in his
theory: "communicative action." Social life involves ongoing linguistic interaction that is dependent upon the continual bondedness of actors to one
another through an implicit set of always operative validity claims. Action
is ongoing and unproblematic when actors at least tacitly accept the particular claims (to truth, rightness, and sincerity) that are presupposed in a
given sequence of their linguistic interaction.[58] Sociologists have traditionally pointed out that normal, ongoing social life is reproduced, at least partially, by the continual transmission of the binding force of shared norms.
What distinguishes Habermas's account of conventional social action is
that it does not—as many earlier accounts did—yield a picture of the self as
a "social dope" who simply conforms to the roles and rules that are operative in the social context. Crucial to Habermas's concept of social action is
the scene of *the self turning upon the other* who has spoken to her *and contesting* some aspect of the underlying claims on the other's part that his
speech is sincere, true, and normatively legitimate. If the more familiar
scene of the ideal speech situation is characterized by the "yeses" that are
elicited from me as I am drawn toward consensus, then this other scene is
characterized by the "noes" that I hurl back at the other and, by so doing,
contest in some way the ongoing normative reproduction of social, economic, and political structures.[59]

This scene thus displays the self's contestation of the other's attempts to keep that self smoothly enfolded in a given set of normative expectations. With this "no," the self both enacts and cites its status as a being with a dignity that demands to be recognized and accorded equal respect. Here we have an ontological scene that can begin to prefigure a normative perspective, on the basis of which we can get some rough distinction between more legitimate and less legitimate modes of political contestation. On its face, however, the scene shows only a kind of blunt opposition. But if we animate it with the core characteristics of human being I have elucidated in the preceding chapters, then a more distinct portrait begins to take shape. The relevant characteristics are capaciousness (freedom and reason), mortal subjectivity (dignity and moral equality), and the articulation of sources of the self in ordinary language. These begin to give minimal shape to certain normative expectations about when respect or recognition has been denied, and thus when that self ought to turn in legitimate opposition.

This ontological scene provides not just direct normative orientation for actors; it also provides a critical perspective from which political inquiry can take its bearings. Critical political theory has been referred to as a "hermeneutic of suspicion" in regard to power and inequality. Habermas's idea of "communicative rationality" provides the normative core of the scene of ongoing linguistic interaction in which an addressee of a speech act turns on the speaker and demands justification. This idealized scene thus provides the criteria from whose perspective a political inquirer can project suspicion onto a given social situation. At issue here especially are situations where there is overt quiescence by actors, but where the inquirer may feel there is some reason for suspecting that the quiescence is an artifact of powerlessness.

I will return to the general issue involved here in a moment, but I first want to be clear about just what I am and am not adopting from Habermas's notion of communicative reason. For my purposes, the ontological scene of opposition provides a vivid representation of the mutual expectations embedded in the interactions of citizens in a democracy. These expectations carry claims of reason that are appropriate to this particular sort of interaction (as opposed to, say, that between a parent and child). But, unlike Habermas, I want to understand these claims as carrying only the force of reasonableness that I have been relying on throughout the book. They do not carry the stronger force of Habermas's full conception of communicative reason that is tied to a stronger idealization of the bonds of reason grounded in a claim about the necessary telos of language.[60] In my terminology, this ties the whole perspective of communicative reason to an unacceptably strong ontology.

Thus my reading of the ontological scene that Habermas gives us will carry less certainty about whether we are fulfilling some telos in the sense of proceeding toward some ideal of justice. And we are certainly not on the road to any specific, determinate account of justice like Rawls's. Rather, one would only hope to roughly recognize situations within which we could identify some harm or injustice. Here I would suggest that we can find a more vivid basis of commonality in our intuitions about harm or *in*justice against which we react, than is the case with the articulation of a clear ideal of justice toward which we ought to move. This approach through a negative solidarity would also seem to be more congruent with that core idea of articulating sources of the self that I have adopted from Taylor. Recall that, for him, sources are articulated slowly, over time, and always remain in some degree of inarticulacy. Given these qualities, it seems sensible to think of negative experience, violations, as having a kind of initial primacy in how we negotiate ethical-political life. In short, my motivation to attend to the activity of articulation, and my sense of the rough direction in which to pursue it, are more plausibly seen as emerging from negative experiences rather than positive ones tied to clear ideals. The ontological scene I have just sketched of the individual turning in opposition to a perceived wrong is intended to capture this intuition.

But, at this point, the critic might object that the foregoing portrait still does not end up giving us much of a critical political viewpoint. She might note that one of the primary philosophical proponents of such a "negative" approach to normativity, namely Richard Rorty, deploys it as a crucial part of what many find to be a relatively *un*critical approach to Western democracies.[61] I don't find this objection persuasive, however, because Rorty's relatively uncritical stance is in no way a necessary conclusion from the negative starting point. That stance only follows if we also give the starting point a particular, and easily resistible, interpretation. For Rorty, the beauty of a negative approach—focusing on harms, especially cruelty—is that it makes normative matters so simple. Everyone knows that cruelty is bad and must be opposed. We need only be made aware of its existence, although becoming adequately informed may require as well some boost to our sympathetic imagination, a task for which "the novel, the movie and the TV program" are the preferred vehicles of education. But this boost is necessary only to call us back to what is, for Rorty, an almost natural moral sensibility. We do not need any philosophical tools when it comes to identifying harms; certainly not those of a political theory that imagines itself as speaking in the name of some claimed, critical standpoint.[62]

But Rorty's desire to "keep it simple," to keep political reflection tied to "banal" insights, betrays too urgent a desire to rid the terrain of ethical-political reflection of all complexity and speculation.[63] Torture would certainly constitute for him an exemplar of easily recognized cruelty. As I suggested in Chapter 4, however, for Americans living in the wake of the events of 9/11 and the Abu Ghraib prisoner abuse scandal, the question of what constitutes torture and whether it should ever be used is anything but simple. My point here is just to suggest that the best approach to the basics of ethical-political reflection is indeed one that starts from negative experiences, but it does not also have to be one that embraces the assumption that such experiences strike us with the clarity and palpableness of being hit with a rock.

What then is required by the task of taking normative complexity more seriously? One crucial aspect involves theoretical speculation about emergent aspects of the ontological scene I introduced above. What if the scene is imagined so that the self *does not turn* in resistance to the normative framework with which he is confronted? That could imply the legitimacy of the norms involved; in short, the self's not turning implies that it tacitly consents to that frame. This presumption might indeed be correct. But Rorty's perspective would have that necessarily be the case. If we allow, however, for a little more complexity in the normative world, we create space for greater critical speculation and suspicion about the meaning of quiescence, or not turning. This is the space where political inquirers might hypothesize about power, and how it may operate in less obtrusive ways than allowed for by Rorty; in short, ways that are not immediately obvious to all the actors. The latter's nonresistance may, for example, reflect the everyday momentum of normalized (in Foucault's sense) social scripts or the failure to comprehend the effects of complex structures of mass media ownership that result in certain sorts of interpretations of events being largely filtered out of the news most citizens receive.[64]

In sum, a radical questioning of power is not prohibited simply because our interpretations of the ethical-political world grow out of a negative starting point. The fact that Rorty does not engage in such questioning reflects concerns of his that are easily separable from his otherwise admirable, initial position regarding the moral experience of the rupture of intersubjective bonds.

6

Conclusion

My efforts in this book have been directed, first, toward introducing the notion of ethos and providing some sense of why its usage in contemporary political discourse has been growing; and, second and more important, toward justifying the exemplary character of a particular ethos for citizens of the wealthy Western democracies. Given the novelty of advocating an ethos, it is worth reviewing and amplifying some of the key claims involved in this endeavor. Toward this end, let me begin by emphasizing what I am *not* doing.

In Chapter 5, I argued for an ethos of democratic citizenship displaying an agonistic respect for others that may show itself in the first instance as a presumptive generosity. Such generosity is intended to be a virtue of limited scope and duration. It does not oblige all actors equally or apply to all situations. And where it does apply, it operates as an initial disposition that may be followed by a variety of more typical political dispositions; say, a willingness to form coalitions or perhaps take up full-scale opposition. So, to forestall the always to be anticipated *reductio ad Hitler,* I must emphasize again that my ethos does not reduce to the recommendation: "Always be generous to Nazis."[1]

Nor does presumptive generosity reduce to the recommendation that in a multicultural world we should embrace "tolerance as [our] dominant political ethos."[2] Tolerance is certainly an important virtue. But it is clearly distinguishable from presumptive generosity. The latter requires from us an at least temporarily more unsettling engagement with the other. It is more unsettling because this ethos expresses an ontological awareness of the way in which political engagement is entangled with the dynamics of identity formation and consolidation. The exercise of tolerance, on the other hand, takes identity as largely set and then worries about the nature of the beliefs and characteristics displayed by the other.[3] Ultimately presumptive generosity requires that I loosen—maybe only minimally and temporarily—the bonds of my identity in encounters with others, especially when they are less privileged than me in an economic or cultural sense.

In the preceding chapter, I also tried to indicate that my turn to ethos does not imply as uncritical an approach to the status quo as is found in Rorty's work, more particularly in his argument that the only angle for critique should be the degree to which a regime prevents cruelty. It is nevertheless the case that I am proposing a kind of cultivation of sensibility that indeed runs parallel to his urging us to expand our sensitivity to the pain and humiliation of others, particularly those who are radically different from us.[4] Given that my project displays this particular affinity, it is especially important for me to delineate further the ways in which my claims depart from Rorty's.

In relation to political thought, Rorty is always determined to keep any emphatic sense of "truth" out of the public sphere. Whether such truth comes in the form of the reason of critical speculation or the commitments of religious faith, its foundationalist claims carry into politics the belief that we can and should transform society in accordance with them. In that way, we can publicly redeem the true meaning of existence and assuage the anxiety of finitude.[5] Against this, Rorty argues that we should give up all emphatic notions of reason and all concern with the foundations of politics. When we do this, we will realize that our efforts to understand human life and finitude belong only in the private sphere. We should be free to "create" and transform ourselves however we wish in private life, but never in public. Even in the private domain, however, we must relinquish any notion that we can "discover" foundations for life; we can only "create" and "recreate" ourselves. In the public sphere, we must rely only on the traditions of freedom in our fortunate democracies that, in turn, will urge upon us the need to progressively cultivate our sensitivity to cruelty.[6]

The ethos I have been advocating runs counter to this series of claims in several ways. First of all, an ethos is explicitly engaged with public life. The virtue of presumptive generosity is to be practiced especially in moments when nascent social movements and ideas begin to push their way into public spheres. What is asked of us as "hosts" in this context is a good deal more demanding than Rorty's "Don't be cruel," as well as differently justified.[7] For Rorty, the maxim of avoiding cruelty is simply self-evident: "pain is nonlinguistic" and thus involves no interpretation or appeal to reason.[8] The idea of presumptive generosity, on the contrary, gains its force from a series of reflections on the form that a reasonable response to the challenges of late modernity might take and how it would be interwoven with the way in which we bear ourselves in an aesthetic-affective fashion. Unlike Rorty's attempt to fully divorce reason and politics, I have tried to sketch a sense of the reasonable that is still emphatic but also chastened by the various twentieth-century critiques of reason.

Such chastening also does not require us to adopt the kind of self-assured antifoundationalism that Rorty embraces. On his view, our most fundamental commitments regarding meaning and finitude are to be understood simply as radical choices we make in a continual process of personal creation and re-creation that is limited only by the "blind impress [of] chance."[9] Rorty scripts those who have attained such an understanding of the world in the role of heroes who boldly face those still mired in the swamp of thinking that their commitments have strong ontological foundations. But I see no compelling reason to buy into such a loaded bipolar representation of the space of late-modern possibility regarding how to bear our most basic commitments in a pluralist world.[10] My ethos is embedded rather in a weak-ontological understanding of sources and their articulation. It draws its sustenance finally from an affirmation of being as a generous presencing or becoming. A disposition of presumptive generosity relates to this presencing in a mimetic way. This mimetic posture has two roles. First, it constitutes a kind of bearing witness to (and thus honoring) the character of being. And, second, it constitutes an initial gesture toward that thin bond of negative solidarity that can take shape among creatures whose dignity and equality reside in their peculiar foreknowledge of mortality.

If the "what" of a late-modern ethos is now clearer, let me reengage the following question: "Who's it for?" It is, as I have repeatedly emphasized, aimed especially at citizens of prosperous democracies that are experiencing the five challenges of late modernity that I have laid out over the course of my chapters. Moreover, it is particularly apt for those in the middle segment of the population. In an economic sense, this middle segment is where a substantial percentage of potential democratic majorities will reside in societies whose distribution of wealth does not look like a pyramid but rather more like a diamond with its bottom point flattened somewhat. The ethos is apt as well for another type of middle; more specifically, the centers of multiple center–periphery relations. These are the extensive centers that exist in terms of ethnicity, race, sexuality, and religion. In the economic middle (especially where it overlaps with one of these hegemonic centers defined in terms of identity), security and well-being often remain shadowed by uncertainty and insecurity. This category of citizens is especially susceptible to the temptation to resentment born of the dynamics of identity/difference. Securing my identity against those marginal "others" who seem to challenge it is an edifying—and usually low-cost—way of tending to public issues.

This mode of resentment differs from the *ressentiment* that Nietzsche made so famous. The latter is a reaction of the weak or powerless against those who dominate them. Nietzsche finds various Jewish and Christian virtues, such as humility, to be the reactive creations of downtrodden religions that wished to get the best, at least symbolically, of their Roman masters.[11] The sort of resentment I have in mind is not one of the strong by the weak but rather of the weak or marginal by the middle. It is a reaction born not of thorough disadvantage but rather of tenuous advantage that seems threatened.

If one now tries to imagine the uptake of a late-modern ethos by individuals in this middle segment of society, a rather large problem begins to push itself forward. I have imagined presumptive generosity as a disposition that is congruent with a kind of nontheism. But isn't the middle segment of American society predominantly theistic in general and Christian in particular? If so, hasn't the number of my potential addressees been thereby radically reduced? There is no denying this. But perhaps there is a way in which presumptive generosity can have an appeal beyond nontheists like myself.

In the Introduction and Chapter 4, I referred to Taylor's effort to think in terms of a Christian ethos grounded in agape, in the sense that an individual's disposition toward others would manifest in a mimetic way God's love for creation. I referred as well to his argument that this sort of ethos has an advantage over nontheistic liberal positions within which the orientation toward others is often directed only by principled imperatives of justice. With nothing more than such principles to direct her public life, the individual may be more likely, Taylor argues, to become easily frustrated with, and hostile toward, the recipients of such actions.[12] Think here of the extraordinarily punitive attitudes of many Americans through the 1970s and 1980s toward welfare recipients, attitudes that radically underestimated the difficulties such recipients faced. Taylor's point is that an ethos sustained by the affirming force of agape will be both more generous and thus more unswervingly committed in its conduct.

It seems to me that there is much to admire in Taylor's argument. But with that strength in his ethos, there also is an associated weakness. Agape has something utterly overwhelming about it, at least when transferred to an expectation placed on humans. The imperfections of the human character may make it too decrepit a vehicle to manifest that love in full and robust form, at least within the everyday life of an ordinary Christian. Taylor has argued persuasively that one result of the Protestant Reformation was that Christianity was increasingly expected to engage more consistently with the everyday lives of ordinary believers, as opposed to the earlier focus on members of religious orders who dedicated their entire lives to their faith.[13] This shift in the character of religion is, in Taylor's view, a central component of the modern Western view of life. But if this is true, it means that the ordinary Christian is not expected to exhibit the same level of devotion as a member of a religious order, a pastor, or a priest.

All I wish to do with this line of reflection is raise the issue of whether Taylor's ethos, rooted in agape, might be put into question—on Taylor's own grounds—as placing too high a demand on the ordinary believer. Now there may be a number of ways within Christian doctrine in which this issue may be artfully managed. I wish only to suggest that a nontheistic, presumptive generosity might be found to overlap rather interestingly with a religious orientation that manifests an *attenuated agape*.

As a way of further illustrating the ethos I am advocating, let me return finally to the controversy over illegal immigration in the United States that I touched on in the Preface. The magnitude and intensity of this topic are clear. As many as fifteen million illegal immigrants (mostly Hispanic) may reside in the United States, amounting to almost five percent of the population. What is to be done in this situation? In late 2007, as the United States headed into an election year, the media were full of proposals designed to play to, and further foster, the kind of resentment to which I have been calling attention. In the space of just two days worth of news, we were warned by a syndicated columnist that "the greatest invasion in history, from the Third World, is swamping the ethno-cultural core of the country"; and we were treated to nationally televised, anti-immigrant sound bites traded by leading presidential candidates.[14]

One accused the other of turning the city of which he had been the mayor into a "sanctuary city" for illegal immigrants, in effect encouraging criminality; the other replied with the charge that his opponent had employed illegals to do yard work, thus turning his home into a "sanctuary mansion."[15]

Such charges would not be so frequent if politicians did not expect to get responses born of resentment that will translate into votes. And not just votes. A movement called the Minutemen (named after the colonial patriots who rapidly assembled to fight the British invasion force around Lexington and Concord at the beginning of the American Revolution) emerged in 2004, exhorting white Americans to arm themselves and hurry south to help patrol the border with Mexico.[16]

How might an ethos of presumptive generosity enter into this caustic environment of red-blooded, American resentment? It does not provide direct answers as to what kind of policy solutions should be adopted. Rather it would encourage more, and more varied, face-to-face engagements of American citizens with immigrants, in order to perhaps better grasp on an everyday level what animates as well as threatens these people's lives. The point would be to slightly dislocate oneself from one's settled identity as host and center. Rom Coles's idea of "moving tables" is deeply suggestive here.[17] Democratic theory often refers us to the right every group has to be at the metaphorical discussion table. Coles urges us rather to think of moving our more privileged selves to the places where the less privileged have their actual tables—in clubs, homes, or churches. The former exchange the role of host at the central discussion table for the role of traveler to less familiar "tables" in less familiar locations. A particularly vivid example of this dislocating orientation is offered in the plan of a small group of citizens from Virginia to travel to Mexico and then follow one of the illegal trails back across the border to the United States.[18]

An ethos of receptive generosity makes no promises about what might happen in such venues. But one can speculate. It seems at least possible that this sort of contact might dampen the tendency to resentment. It is interesting that surveys find that Americans are highly resentful when confronted with an influx of "faceless newcomers," but become less so when faced with specific cases: "We fear the hordes, while we welcome the family."[19] The late-modern ethos I recommend would aim in such a symbolically charged atmosphere at cultivating a sensibility that sees individuals, families, and ways of life, not collective types.

Finally, I need to say a word about the role an appeal to reason plays in this book. I have sketched out an ethos of citizenship that takes shape around "reasonable" responses to the key challenges of late modernity. Some may find this appeal to reason to be ill advised. This worry is nicely summed up by Raymond Geuss: "a major danger in using highly abstractive methods in political philosophy is that one will succeed merely in generalizing one's own local prejudices and repackaging them as demands of reason."[20] There is indeed danger in any sort of normative abstraction employed by political theorists; and this should never be glossed over. But there are potential benefits as well, one of the most important of which is maintaining a strand of continuity in Western political thought. I have chosen to undertake a balancing act with regard to reason, calling my conception "emphatic, but chastened." My sense is that one cannot know at the beginning of such a project whether the dangers have been poorly assessed versus the benefits. Good judgment must wait until the project is fleshed out. In this case, one must see if the idea of a late-modern ethos is in fact persuasive, or whether it carries insufficiently acknowledged dangers of the sort Geuss rightly highlights.

Perhaps then the question is not really one with a simple, dichotomous choice of answers: use an emphatic conception of reason or forgo entirely any such appeal. Rather the real question is the following: Which option best balances dangers and benefits, all things considered? Late-modern political theory might be compared to a peculiar circus in which the only good acts are good balancing acts.

Notes

1. Introduction

1. Aristotle, *Aristotle: On Rhetoric,* ed. and trans. George A. Kennedy, 2d ed. (New York: Oxford University Press, 2007). Aristotle contends that three means of persuasion operate in speech: persuasion through reason (logos); persuasion by the character, or more specifically, the moral character of the speaker (ethos); and finally, persuasion that operates purely on the emotions of the hearer (pathos). The establishment of one's *ethos*—uprightness or trustworthiness—in public speech is not immediately dependent upon the reputation you have or position of authority you hold; rather it seems peculiarly dependent upon how the speaker's virtue can be manifested by both his affective bearing and the fairness of his arguments. Thus we see that ethos is peculiarly aligned with both practical reason and affect, or emotion. See pp. 37–39, 39n41.

The definition of *ethos* in the *OED* as community sentiment seems to invoke the idea of a collective sharing more strongly than Aristotle's. But this difference probably should not be overstated, because Aristotle's emphasis on the individual's cultivation of character is not divorced from the general character ideals of a Greek citizen.

2. For a sample of recent usages of *ethos,* see James Tully, "Political Philosophy as a Critical Activity," in *What Is Political Theory?* ed. Stephen K. White and J. Donald Moon (Thousand Oaks, Calif.: Sage Publications, 2004), p. 98; William Connolly, *The Ethos of Pluralism* (Minneapolis: University of Minnesota Press, 1995); Richard Bernstein, "The Retrieval of a Democratic Ethos," in *Habermas on Law and Democracy,* ed. Michael Rosenfeld and Andrew Arato (Berkeley: University of California Press, 1998); Wendy Brown, *Regulating Aversion: Tolerance in the Age of Identity and Empire* (Princeton, N.J.: Princeton University Press, 2006), pp. 16, 87–88; Chantal Mouffe, "Deconstruction, Pragmatism and the Politics of Democracy," in *Deconstruction and Pragmatism* (London: Routledge, 1996), p. 5; and Amanda Anderson, *The Way We Argue Now: A Study in the Cultures of Theory* (Princeton, N.J.: Princeton University Press, 2006), pp. 1–17, 134–160.

Although *ethos* appears most frequently in the work of scholars who are influenced by the continental tradition of political thought, it has also begun to make its appearance in analytical philosophy; see G. A. Cohen, *If You're an Egalitarian, How Come You're So Rich?* (Cambridge, Mass.: Harvard University Press, 2000), chaps. 7–9.

Ethos is being used increasingly in official public discourse as well popular culture. For an example of official usage in public discourse, see the state of Virginia's 2007 resolution of "profound regret" for slavery: "WHEREAS, to prime Africans for slavery, the ethos of the Africans was shattered . . ." at http://www.leg1.state.va .us (accessed 8/26/07). In popular culture, a socially conscious bottled water company has taken the name "Ethos Water." In spring 2008, it was prominently displayed in Starbucks coffee shops with a note that the company contributes a few cents from each bottle to insure that impoverished children around the world have access to clean water.

3. Michel Foucault, "The Ethics of the Concern of the Self as a Practice of Freedom," in *The Essential Foucault: Selections from 'The Essential Works of Foucault 1954–1984,'* ed. P. Rabinow and Nikolas Rose (New York: New Press, 2003), pp. 28–30; and "Politics and Ethics: An Interview," in *The Foucault Reader,* ed. Paul Rabinow (New York: Pantheon, 1984), pp. 373–377.

As with the ancient Greeks, Foucault attends to *ethos* at both the individual and collective levels. He tends to focus more on modes of individual cultivation; at the same time, however, the whole notion of ethos is drawn into his work as a useful vehicle for speaking broadly about practical reason.

4. Foucault, "Politics and Ethics," p. 377.

5. Jean-Francois Lyotard, *The Postmodern Condition: A Report on Knowledge,* trans. G. Bennington and B. Massumi (Minneapolis: University of Minnesota Press, 1984), p. xxiv.

6. Richard Rorty, "Habermas and Lyotard on Postmodernity," in *Philosophical Papers,* vol. 2, *Essays on Heidegger and Others* (Cambridge: Cambridge University Press, 1991), pp. 167, 176.

7. This kind of response to postmodernist claims is really just an updating of Leo Strauss's critique of "historicism" as leading to "nihilism"; *Natural Right and History* (Chicago: University of Chicago Press, 1953), pp. 5–6.

8. Stephen K. White, *Sustaining Affirmation: The Strengths of Weak Ontology* (Princeton, N.J.: Princeton University Press, 2000), chap. 1; and Charles Taylor, *Sources of the Self: The Making of Modern Identity* (Cambridge, Mass.: Harvard University Press, 1989).

9. For a discussion of how the figures of a weak ontology "prefigure" our ethical-political commitments, see my *Sustaining Affirmation,* pp. 6–12.

10. Foucault's use of *ethos* seems to parallel Heidegger's in regard to its critical stance toward mainstream, modern understandings of both ethics and practical reason. See Martin Heidegger, "Letter on Humanism," in *Martin Heidegger: Basic Writings,* ed. and trans. David Farrell Krell (New York: Harper and Row, 1977), pp. 232–235.

11. Amanda Anderson, *The Way We Argue Now*, 2006), pp. 7–12. Anderson tries to get beyond this split between reason and ethos by proposing what she calls "an ethos *of* reason and argument" (p. 17) (my emphasis). She urges us to adopt the virtues and affects that constitute a "spirit of proceduralism," in effect bringing us to see "argument as ethos" (pp. 156, 179–181, 186). I criticize this approach to the question of ethos in "The Self-Understanding of Political Theory Today," *Political Theory* 34:6 (December 2006): 785–790.

12. My reference to charges of "postmodern irrationalism" does not imply that I would condemn all that passes as "postmodern" or defend it.

13. My sense is that the German phrase *Sei Vernunftig* is quite similar in meaning.

14. Alessandro Ferrara, *The Force of the Example: Explorations in the Paradigm of Judgment* (New York: Columbia University Press, 2008).

15. Ibid., pp. 20-21, 79.

16. Taylor, *Sources of the Self,* chap. 25. See my discussion of these issues in *Sustaining Affirmation,* chap. 3.

17. Wendy Brown, *Edgework: Critical Essays on Knowledge and Politics* (Princeton, N.J.: Princeton University Press, 2005), pp. 22–23, 35–36. Although she urges us to embrace this ethos of civic love, she also worries that at least some sorts of ethe will be taken up for the wrong sort of reason, namely, as a vehicle for "appeasing left despair about the contemporary non-viability of a radical democratic perspective"; see Brown, "Democracy and Bad Dreams," *Theory & Event* 10:1 (2007): para. 18.

18. I intentionally use the description *nontheistic* to characterize my position. My reason for not using a more familiar term such as *atheistic* is that I do not claim that I know there is no God, as is the case with atheists. From my weak-ontological position, I could not be in the position to know such a thing for certain. I take an agonistic position on all such strong ontological claims. But this does not mean that I am simply agonistic on all fundamental claims. Rather I affirm a weak-ontological account of being as *presencing* or *becoming*. What that means exactly should become clearer as the text progresses.

19. None of the ethe I have just mentioned, including mine, attends adequately to what must become a major point of further emendation for them all in the future: articulating a way of tending appropriately to the environmental challenges we face.

20. For an excellent treatment of Diderot on empire, see Sankar Muthu, *Enlightenment against Empire* (Princeton, N.J.: Princeton University Press, 2003), chap. 3.

21. For this list of liberal virtues, see Stephen Macedo, "Transformative Constitutionalism and the Case of Religion: Defending the Moderate Hegemony of Liberalism," *Political Theory* (February 1998): 59.

22. Although I am putting special emphasis here on "distant others" in a global context, I intend for it to extend as well to different sorts of nongeographical distance, such as cultural, economic, racial, or sexual.

23. The argument that societies such as that of the United States are shaped more like a diamond than a pyramid is contained in Robert Perrucci and Earl Wysong, *The New Class Society: Goodbye to the American Dream?* (Lanham, Md.: Rowman and Littlefield, 2003), chap. 1. I have added the qualification that the bottom point of the diamond is ground down somewhat simply to emphasize that the very poorest category does not constitute a minuscule group. I don't think Perrucci and Wysong would disagree. Additionally, they contend that this diamond has a smaller one perched on top of it, indicating a certain character of the distribution of wealth among the most fortunate segments of the U.S. population. For my purposes, I am only interested in the shape of the bottom of the figure.

2. Reason and Ethos

1. For a classic attempt to reduce the problem of the social contract to a collective action problem resolvable purely through strategic rationality, see James Buchanan and Gordon Tullock, eds., *The Calculus of Consent: Logical Foundations of Constitutional Democracy* (Ann Arbor: University of Michigan Press, 1962).

2. Theodor Adorno uses the term *emphatic (nachdrucklich)* in a somewhat similar way in *Negative Dialectics,* trans. E. B. Ashton (New York: Continuum, 1966), pp. 24, 150–151.

3. See the cover illustration of James Schmidt, ed., *What Is Enlightenment? Eighteenth Century Answers and Twentieth Century Questions* (Berkeley: University of California Press, 1996).

4. Max Horkheimer and Theodor Adorno, *Dialectic of Enlightenment: Philosophical Fragments,* ed. Gunzelin Schmid Noerr, trans. Edmund Jephcott (1947; reprint, Stanford, Calif.: Stanford University Press, 2002). For Heidegger, see Martin Heidegger, "Letter on Humanism" and "The Question Concerning Technology," in *Martin Heidegger: Basic Writings,* ed. and trans. David Farrell Krell (New York: Harper and Row, 1977). The first essay was originally published in 1947; the second was first given as a lecture in 1949 and published in a revised form in 1954. For Foucault, see especially Michel Foucault, *Discipline and Punish: The Birth of the Prison,* trans. Alan Sheridan (New York: Vintage, 1979). See also William Connolly, "The Politics of Discourse," in *The Terms of Political Discourse,* 3d ed. (Princeton, N.J.: Princeton University Press, 1993), pp. 213–243; and *Identity/Difference: Democratic Negotiations of Political Paradox,* 2d ed. (Minneapolis: University of Minnesota Press, 2003).

5. See my *Edmund Burke: Modernity, Politics, and Aesthetics,* 2d ed. (Lanham, Md.: Rowman and Littlefield, 2002), chap. 4.

6. Foucault, *Discipline and Punish,* p. 139.

7. Ibid., pt. 3.

8. See, for example, Foucault, "What Is Enlightenment?" trans. C. Porter, and "Politics and Ethics: An Interview," *The Foucault Reader,* pp. 32–50, 373–380; and Horkheimer and Adorno, *Dialectic of Enlightenment,* p. xviii.

9. John Rawls, *Political Liberalism* (New York: Columbia University Press, 1993), pp. 48–81. I refer to Rawls's account of justice here as "late modern," because it starts from certain lessons he claims we have learned in "a modern democratic society," p. xvi.

10. Ibid., pp. 9–10.

11. This point is well argued by Charles Taylor, "The Politics of Recognition," in *Multiculturalism: Examining the Politics of Recognition,* ed. Amy Gutmann (Princeton, N.J.: Princeton University Press, 1994), pp. 25–73.

12. Rawls, *Political Liberalism,* pp. 17–18, 36ff.

13. Ibid., pp. 10–11, 54–60.

14. Ibid., pp. 54–58, 81.

15. Charles Larmore, "The Moral Basis of Liberalism," *Journal of Philosophy* 96:12 (December 1999): 599–625; and "Respect for Persons," in "Commitments in a Post-Foundationalist World: Exploring the Possibilities of 'Weak Ontology,'" special issue, *Hedgehog Review* 7:2 (Summer 2005): 66–76.

16. Larmore, "Respect for Persons," p. 71; and "Moral Basis of Liberalism," pp. 601–602, 607–608.

17. Larmore, "Respect for Persons," p. 75.

18. Larmore, "Moral Basis of Liberalism," pp. 606–609; and "Respect for Persons," p. 75.

19. Rawls, "Overlapping Consensus," *Oxford Journal of Legal Studies* 7:1 (February 1987): 14.

20. Rawls, *Political Liberalism,* pp. xvi, 8.

21. Ibid., pp. 11–12, and Lecture VII.

22. Charles Taylor, *Philosophical Arguments* (Cambridge, Mass.: Harvard University Press, 1995), p. xii.

23. Compare here G. A. Cohen's critique of Rawls's theory of justice. He contends that the force of principles of justice extends not just to obeying the rules related to basic structures but also to the everyday choices that help reproduce those structures over time. When such choices are an object of concern, then one must accept as well that justice demands that we affirm an ethos that draws those choices toward what is demanded by principles of justice. See *If You're an Egalitarian, How Come You're So Rich?* pp. x, 120, 123–147.

24. J. S. Mill, *'On Liberty' and Other Writings,* ed. Stefan Collini (Cambridge: Cambridge University Press, 1989), pp. 8–9.

25. Jürgen Habermas, *Between Facts and Norms: Contributions to a Theory of Law and Democracy,* trans. William Rehg (Cambridge, Mass.: MIT Press, 1996).

26. Taylor, *Sources of the Self,* p. 505.

27. The second, broader sense of *finitude* is meant to include insights such as not having the time or capacity to satisfy all of my desires and knowing that when I make a major decision in life, I cannot later revisit that decision point in exactly the same way as the first time, only this time choosing differently.

28. Richard Rorty explicitly casts the whole question of foundations as a stark, dichotomous issue of discovery or choice; see his *Contingency, Irony and Solidarity* (Cambridge: Cambridge University Press, 1989), pp. 27, 42–43.

29. Here I am following Taylor, *Sources of the Self*, pp. 30–32, 331–332.

30. Ibid., pp. 8–9, 91–96.

31. Ibid., pp. 18, 22, 34, 334, 419.

32. Taylor draws some of his sense of human being figured as a quest from Alasdair MacIntyre; see his *After Virtue: A Study of Moral Theory* (Notre Dame, Ind.: University of Notre Dame Press, 1981), pp. 203–206. This is true to a degree, but the sense of a quest that emerges in the articulation model is not set against MacIntyre's stark master narrative of late modernity as "the new dark ages which is already upon us" (245). Such a division of the world into light and dark threatens to swallow up the more engaging implications of the idea of life as a deeply uncertain sort of journey.

33. Rawls, *Political Liberalism*, pp. 54–61.

34. Ibid., pp. 58–64.

35. Quoted in Peter Ford, "Europe Cringes at Bush's 'Crusade' against Terrorists," *Christian Science Monitor*, September 19, 2001, http://www.csmonitor.com/2001/0919/p12s2-woeu.html (accessed on 2/14/06).

36. For a view that makes finitude a secondary matter, consider the way the idea of the "Rapture" seems to function today among some Protestant fundamentalists in the United States.

37. When I refer to *theism*, I am speaking of Christianity; how my thoughts extend to other religions is left open.

38. John Woolman, *The Journal and Major Essays of John Woolman*, ed. Phillips P. Moulton (Richmond, Ind.: Friends United Press, 1971), p. 93.

39. The way I am deploying this distinction between "deepest commitment" and "absolute conviction" seems to me to be close to Taylor's efforts to talk about religious belief and unbelief in a way that sees them less "as rival *theories*" than as "different kinds of lived experience" or "alternative ways of living our moral/spiritual life, in the broadest sense." See his *A Secular Age* (Cambridge, Mass.: Harvard University Press, 2007), pp. 4–5, 8, 11.

40. Ibid., p. 127.

41. I borrow the use of *pilgrim* from Richard Falk, although the content I am assigning to a nontheistic, late-modern pilgrim differs from his "citizen pilgrim"; "An Emergent Matrix of Citizenship: Complex, Uneven and Fluid," in *Global Citizenship: A Critical Reader*, ed. Nigel Dower and John Williams (Edinburgh: Edinburgh University Press, 2002), pp. 26–28.

42. The issue of subjection to mortality and its role in a late-modern ethics will be fleshed out further in Chapter 4.

43. Taylor, *Sources of the Self*, p. 27.

44. For some general sense of the debates, see Taylor, "The Politics of Recognition"; Patchen Markell, *Bound by Recognition* (Chicago: University of Chicago

Press, 2003); and Alain-G. Gagnon and James Tully, eds., *Multinational Democracies* (Cambridge: Cambridge University Press, 2001).

45. See Muthu, *Enlightenment against Empire,* for an excellent treatment of the diversity of views among Enlightenment thinkers in regard to how they did or did not associate reason and freedom with the legitimacy of empire.

46. Judith Butler, *Gender Trouble* : Feminism and the Subversion of Identity (New York: Routledge, 1990).

47. Butler, "The Force of Fantasy: Feminism, Mapplethorpe, and Discursive Excess," *Differences* 2:2 (1990): 121.

48. Nancy Fraser, "False Antitheses: A Response to Seyla Benhabib and Judith Butler," in *Feminist Contentions: A Philosophical Exchange,* by Seyla Benhabib, Judith Butler, Drucilla Cornell, and Nancy Fraser (New York: Routledge, 1995), p. 71. For a discussion of how Butler has overcome this problem in later work, see my *Sustaining Affirmation,* chap. 4.

49. Markell, *Bound by Recognition,* p. 23. He calls this "the Penelope problem."

50. William Connolly, *Identity/Difference,* especially the introduction.

51. Ibid., pp. 8–9, 64.

52. Ibid., pp. 9, 16–20, 29–32; and *The Ethos of Pluralization* (Minneapolis: University of Minnesota Press, 1995), pp. 16–20. He finds that the temptation also grows in the context of religious attitudes of attunement.

53. Mill, *'On Liberty' and Other Writings;* at one point, Mill calls intolerance more "natural" than tolerance; p. 11.

54. Ibid., p. 13.

55. The force of this portrait is supported by empirical research; see John R. Hibbing and Elizabeth Theiss-Morse, *Stealth Democracy: Americans' Beliefs about How Government Should Work* (Cambridge: Cambridge University Press, 2002), pp. 105–106, 134–135, 149–150, 156–157, 221–223. Americans tend to be "conflict averse" and deeply suspicious of amorphous "others" who seem to foment disagreement that disturbs the deep consensus the former believe (incorrectly) characterizes the American population.

56. Connolly, *The Ethos of Pluralization,* pp. 178–188; Jacques Derrida and Anne Dufourmantelle, *Of Hospitality* (Stanford, Calif.: Stanford University Press, 2000); Romand Coles, *Rethinking Generosity: Critical Theory and the Politics of Caritas* (Ithaca, N.Y.: Cornell University Press, 1997), p. 23; Patchen Markell, *Bound by Recognition,* pp. 14–15, 32–36; and Judith Butler, "For a Careful Reading," in *Feminist Contentions,* p. 140. Butler uses *capaciousness* differently than I do. My usage picks out views of human being focused primarily on exercising the capacities of freedom and reason, whereas she is using it in a broader sense.

57. In an earlier work, I tried to grapple with this whole issue through the concept of a "lightness of care"; *Political Theory and Postmodernism* (Cambridge: Cambridge University Press, 1991), pp. xi, 90–113, 125, 128, 137.

58. Connolly, *Identity/Difference,* pp. 8–9.

3. After Critique

1. In saying that Schmitt's portrait of a postliberal politics is a deeply fascist one, I do not mean to imply that Heidegger had no connection to Nazism. My point is merely that Schmitt wrote on more overtly political subjects and in a more clearly fascist way.

2. A good sense of the current Schmitt controversy can be gotten from Tracy Strong's foreword to *The Concept of the Political*, by Carl Schmitt, trans. and intro. George Schwab (Chicago: University of Chicago Press, 1996); and the essays in *The Challenge of Carl Schmitt*, ed. Chantal Mouffe (London: Verso Books, 1999).

3. Schmitt, *Concept of the Political*, pp. 27–28.

4. Mouffe, introduction to *Challenge of Carl Schmitt*, p. 4; and "Carl Schmitt and the Paradox of Liberal Democracy," in *Challenge of Carl Schmitt*, p. 43.

5. Mouffe, *On the Political* (London: Routledge, 2005), pp. 19–21; and introduction to *Challenge of Carl Schmitt*, p. 4.

6. Mouffe, *On the Political*, pp. 19–20; and introduction to *Challenge of Carl Schmitt*, pp. 4–5.

7. Mouffe, *On the Political*, pp. 24–25.

8. Mouffe, "Carl Schmitt and the Paradox," *Challenge of Carl Schmitt*, pp. 43–44.

9. Connolly is, to my knowledge, the one who introduced the term *agonistic democracy*. See *Identity/Difference*, p. x.

10. See especially Connolly, *Ethos of Pluralization*; as well as my *Sustaining Affirmation*, chap. 5.

11. Schmitt, *Concept of the Political*, p. 79.

12. Ibid., p. 27.

13. Mouffe, *On the Political*, p. 14.

14. Ibid., p. 3; and Mouffe, introduction to *Challenge of Carl Schmitt*, p. 6.

15. Friedrich Nietzsche, "Homer on Competition," in *On the Genealogy of Morality*, ed. Keith Ansell-Pearson, trans. Carol Diethe (Cambridge: Cambridge University Press, 1994), pp. 187–194.

16. Ibid., pp. 192–193.

17. Ibid., pp. 191–192.

18. Connolly, *Identity/Difference*, pp. xi–x, 8–9, 64.

19. See my discussion of Connolly's ontology in terms of this Heideggerian idea in *Sustaining Affirmation*, pp. 108–113.

20. Connolly, *The Augustinian Imperative* (Newbury Park, Calif.: Sage Publications, 1993), p. 141.

21. See John Rawls, *Political Liberalism*; Charles Larmore, *Patterns of Moral Complexity* (Cambridge: Cambridge University Press, 1987); *The Morals of Modernity* (Cambridge: Cambridge University Press, 1996); and J. Donald Moon, *Constructing Community: Moral Pluralism and Tragic Conflicts* (Princeton, N.J.: Princeton University Press, 1993).

22. Rawls, *Political Liberalism*, pp. 36–38; Larmore, *Patterns of Moral Complexity*, p. 43.

23. Immanuel Kant, *Groundwork of the Metaphysics of Morals*, trans. and ed. Mary Gregor, intro. Christine M. Korsgaard (Cambridge: Cambridge University Press, 1997), pp. 22–23, 35, 46, 48–49.

24. I am drawing on Edmund Burke's conception of the sublime in *A Philosophical Enquiry into the Origin of Our Ideas of the Sublime and Beautiful* (Oxford: Oxford University Press, 1990), pt. 1, sec. 7.

25. Kant, *Groundwork*, pp. xxviii–xxix, 45, 56–57.

26. Mary Ann Glendon, *A World Made New: Eleanor Roosevelt and the Declaration of Human Rights* (New York: Random House), p. 147; and John Locke, "The Second Treatise of Government," in *Two Treatises of Government*, chap. 2, para. 6.

27. Larmore, *Patterns of Moral Complexity*, pp. 62–63.

28. I raise some problems for Larmore's position here; others are raised in the next chapter.

29. Kant, *Groundwork*, pp. 13–14, 42–42, 46.

30. Cohen, *If You Are an Egalitarian, How Come You're So Rich?* pp. 3-6, 123.

31. See Wendy Brown for an interesting discussion of how the object of tolerance has shifted from belief to identity; *Regulating Aversion*, pp. 34–47.

32. J. S. Mill, *'On Liberty' and Other Writings*, p. 11.

33. Ibid., p. 14.

34. Connolly, *IdentityDifference*, pp. 73–75; and *The Ethos of Pluralization*, pp. 16–17.

35. In an earlier version of this essay, I tried to articulate a sense of human dignity that, mistakenly, did not include the quality of being conscious of finitude as a crucial component; see "After Critique: Affirming Subjectivity in Contemporary Political Thought," *European Journal of Political Theory* 3:2 (April 2003): 223–224.

36. See my discussion of this concept in *Edmund Burke: Modernity, Politics, and Aesthetics*, pp. 68–79.

4. Animating the Reach of Our Moral Imagination

1. Sometimes critics suggest that today too much emphasis is put on issues of agonism and difference, minority rights, multiculturalism, and so on. But evidence seems to be accumulating that we will never be able to settle back into old, comfortable assumptions about unitary states with their undifferentiated citizenry. As Will Kymlicka writes: "In the past, countries with robust minority rights were often seen as 'exceptions', if not 'deviations', from what a 'normal' state looks like . . . In recent years, however, international organizations have revised their views [and] literally reversed the tables. In contemporary international discourse, the idea of a centralized, unitary, and homogenous state is increasingly described as an anachronism, a

throwback to the nineteenth century"; *Multicultural Odysseys: Navigating the New International Politics of Diversity* (Oxford: Oxford University Press, 2007), p. 42.

2. Let me emphasize again that I am confining myself to theism in the Christian tradition.

3. David Hollinger, "Debates with the PTA and Others," in *Human Rights as Politics and Idolatry*, by Michael Ignatieff, ed. and intro. Amy Gutmann (Princeton, N.J.: Princeton University Press, 2001), pp. 125–126.

4. John Locke, *Second Treatise of Government*, chap. 2, para. 6.

5. Jeremy Waldron, *God, Locke and Equality: Christian Foundations in Locke's Political Thought* (Cambridge: Cambridge University Press, 2003), pp. 12–14, 44–45, 81–82. See also his "Response to Critics," *Review of Politics* 76 (2005): 495–513.

6. Jack Donnelly, *Universal Human Rights in Theory and Practice*, 2d ed. (Ithaca, N.Y.: Cornell University Press, 2003), p. 10. Cf. Michael Ignatieff, "Human Rights as Politics," in *Human Rights*, pp. 3–4.

7. Waldron, *God, Locke and Equality*, pp. 71–72, 75–81.

8. Taylor, *Sources of the Self*, 495-521.

9. Ibid., pp. 515–517.

10. Ibid., p. 516.

11. *Sustaining Affirmation*, pp. 147–148.

12. Taylor, *Sources of the Self*, pp. 316–317.

13. See, for example, Quentin Skinner, "Modernity and Disenchantment: Some Historical Reflections," in *Philosophy in an Age of Pluralism*, ed. James Tully (Cambridge: Cambridge University Press, 1994), pp. 46–47; and Ignatieff, "Human Rights as Idolatry," in *Human Rights*, pp. 86–87.

14. Donnelly, *Universal Human Rights*, pp. 17–21. The idea of a consensus on such things as torture has, of course, been clouded by the policy of the Bush administration toward detainees in the United States' "war on terror." I will return to this topic later in the chapter.

15. Amy Gutmann, introduction to *Human Rights*, by Ignatieff, p. xix. It is important to see that appeals to "overlapping consensus" can in fact be quite varied in terms of their philosophical content. For example, both Gutmann and Charles Taylor make such an appeal, but they have in mind different overall notions as to what is the subject of such a consensus. See Taylor, "Conditions of an Unforced Consensus on Human Rights," in *The East Asian Challenge for Human Rights*, ed. Joanne R. Bauer and Daniel Bell (Cambridge: Cambridge University Press, 1999), pp. 124–144; and *Sources of the Self*, pp. 515–516. A variation of this strategy is recommended by Richard Rorty. However, his suggestion that we ignore foundational issues is joined to the idea that we should substitute attention to "sentimental education." Although I think he is onto something with the latter recommendation, I would argue that it can be combined with the notion of weak ontological reflection; Rorty, "Human Rights, Rationality and Sentimentality," in *Philosophical Papers*, vol. 3, *Truth and Progress* (Cambridge: Cambridge University Press, 1998), pp. 180–181.

16. Ignatieff, "Human Rights as Idolatry," in *Human Rights,* pp. 82–85. Ignatieff's argument is one variation on the strategy of "overlapping consensus." He asks us not to delve into foundations, but rather to stick to the simple idea of agency plus the historical lesson that human rights are necessary to protect the autonomy of the agent; pp. 55–57, 83–34. In her introduction to this book, Amy Gutmann finds fault with such an approach to "overlapping consensus," pp. xvi–xix.

17. Ignatieff, "Response to Commentators," in *Human Rights,* pp. 163–165.

18. Ibid., pp. 164–165, 169, 171.

19. See, for example, Max Stackhouse, "Human Rights and Public Theology: The Basic Validation of Human Rights," in *Religion and Human Rights: Competing Claims?* ed. Carrie Gustafson and Peter Juviler (Armonk, N.Y.; M. E. Sharpe, 1999), pp. 12–27; and Michael J. Perry, *The Idea of Human Rights: Four Inquiries* (Oxford: Oxford University Press, 1998), chap. 1.

20. John Rawls, *Political Liberalism.*

21. Rawls considers issues of global justice and human rights in *The Law of Peoples* (Cambridge, Mass.: Harvard University Press, 1999).

22. Larmore, "Respect for Persons," p. 71.

23. Ibid., pp. 75–76.

24. Larmore does admit, however, that in our "bio-engineering future," practices may emerge that will open this commitment to doubt; ibid., p. 77.

25. See Mark Danner, *Torture and the Truth: America, Abu Ghraib, and the War on Terror* (New York: New York Review Books, 2004).

26. President Bush characterized the problem at Abu Ghraib this way in an interview with the Al Arabiya television network on May 5, 2004.

27. For a summary of research in this area, see J. L. Sullivan and J. C. Transue, "The Psychological Underpinnings of Democracy: A Selective Review of Research on Political Tolerance, Interpersonal Trust, and Social Capital," *Annual Review of Psychology* 50 (February 1999): 625–650.

28. For examples of Bush's persistent use of the language of evil, see his speeches on 9/11, 9/12 ("This will be a monumental struggle of good versus evil, but good will prevail"), and 9/13, http://www.americanrhetoric.com (accessed 6/7/08). Up until February 2004, the Web page for the USA Freedom Corps, Bush's new umbrella organization for volunteerism, featured a photograph of President Bush surrounded by small children; the banner next to it called citizens to "love someone, mentor a child, stand up to evil . . ."; http://www.usafreedomcorps.gov.

29. Waldron, *God, Locke and Equality,* p. 81.

30. Ibid., p. 77.

31. *The OED* illustrates this sense of *subjection* with a quotation from T. Spencer in 1628: "His subjection to death; as a quality of his being."

32. See Oliver Sensen, "How Human Dignity Grounds Human Rights" (paper, Mid-West Political Science Convention, Chicago, April 2005), pp. 14–16.

33. Ignatieff, "Response to Commentators," in *Human Rights,* p. 163.

34. Taylor, *Sources of the Self,* pt. 1.

35. See the interesting discussion of Luther's dread of death in Richard Marius, *Martin Luther: The Christian between God and Death* (Cambridge, Mass.: Harvard University Press, 1999), pp. 59ff.

36. Albert Camus, "The Myth of Sisyphus," in *The Myth of Sisyphus and Other Essays,* trans. Justin O'Brien (New York: Random House, 1955), pp. 88–91.

37. Connolly, *Identity/Difference,* especially the introduction and chap. 1.

38. A rough parallel exists between my sense of how we might configure the relation between pain and mortality and Edmund Burke's understanding of "pain . . . as an emissary of this king of terrors"; *A Philosophical Enquiry,* p. 36.

39. Judith Butler, *Precarious Life: The Powers of Mourning and Violence* (London: Verso, 2004), pp. 20–23.

40. Bryan Turner, *Vulnerability and Human Rights* (University Park, Penn.: Pennsylvania State University Press, 2006). Perhaps the most prominent representative of the appeal to vulnerability is Rorty. See his *Contingency, Irony and Solidarity,* pp. xv–xvi, 87–94.

41. Ibid., pp. 1, 13, 27–29, 35. Turner's claim about the universality of pain seems to be identical to Rorty's. The latter finds vulnerability to pain to be beyond interpretation in a certain sense because "pain is nonlinguistic"; *Contingency, Irony and Solidarity,* pp. 88, 94.

42. Turner, *Vulnerability,* p. 29.

43. Burke, *A Philosophical Enquiry,* p. 36.

44. Turner, *Vulnerability,* p. 1.

45. Ibid., p. 27.

46. Ignatieff, "Response to Commentators," *Human Rights,* p. 163.

47. The notion that death cuts through everything else in a distinctive fashion that reveals our "mere humanity" is nicely captured by G. K. Chesterton: "We should say, after a somewhat disturbing discovery, 'There is a dead man under the sofa.' We should not be likely to say, 'There is a dead man of considerable personal refinement under the sofa' . . . Nobody would say 'There are the remains of a clear thinker in your back garden.'" Gilbert K. Chesterton, *Heretics* (Freeport, N.Y.: Books for Libraries Press, 1970), pp. 272–273. I thank Sara Henary for bringing my attention to this passage.

48. This characterization of contemporary affluent societies should not be taken to imply that there is no problem of moral attentiveness to misery *within* those societies. We see this in measures such as infant mortality. The United States, for example, despite its huge wealth nevertheless ranks forty-second in its rate of infant mortality. See the Central Intelligence Agency, "Rank Order—Infant Mortality Rate," in *The World Factbook,* http://www.cia.gov/library/publications/the-world-factbook (accessed on April 19, 2008).

49. On the connection between respect and status, see Bird, "Status, Identity and Respect," *Political Theory* 32:2 (April 2004): 207–232.

50. Although Jürgen Habermas comes at agency from the intersubjective viewpoint of "communicative rationality," one can see the kind of claim I am attributing to defenders of capacious agency in his suggestion that "the sole source of solidarity among strangers" is constituted by their possible "communicative mastery" of conflicts; see Habermas, *Between Facts and Norms*, p. 308.

51. Rorty also wants to open up the basis for possible human solidarity by looking to a shared *negative* quality or experience: the vulnerability to pain and humiliation. Our "sense of human solidarity is based on a sense of a common danger, not on a common possession or shared power"; *Contingency, Irony and Solidarity*, p. 91.

52. This commonality is too slender, by itself, to generate a sense of connectedness strong enough to sustain a continuing sense of ethical-political obligation. For that to occur, one needs to manifest as well some minimal responsiveness to the expectation of reasonableness that is neither theistically informed, such as Locke's, nor stripped down to some form of strategic reason, such as Hobbes's.

53. Peter Euben expressed this criticism to me in personal communication.

54. Bernard Knox suggests that we should always keep in mind that the theme of *The Iliad*, the "mainspring of the plot," is stated in the opening line: "Rage—Goddess, sing the rage of Peleus' son Achilles." Accordingly, anything that shows itself capable of standing up to the force of this mainspring would seem to be especially significant. See Homer, *The Iliad*, trans. Robert Fagles, intro. and notes Bernard Knox (Harmondsworth, U.K.: Penguin Books, 1990), p. 3.

5. Democracy's Predicament

1. See, for example, Sheldon Wolin, *Politics and Vision*, 2d ed. (Princeton, N.J.: Princeton University Press, 2004), pp. xvi, 578–606; Jacques Derrida, *Specters of Marx: The State of the Debt, the Work of Mourning and the New International*, trans. Peggy Kamuf, intro. Bernd Magnus and Stephen Cullenberg (New York: Routledge, 1994), pp. 59, 75; Wendy Brown, "American Nightmare: Neoliberalism, Neoconservatism, and De-democratization," *Political Theory* 34:6 (December 2006): 690–714; and "Untimeliness and Punctuality: Critical Theory in Dark Times," in *Edgework: Critical Essays in Knowledge and Politics* (Princeton, N.J.: Princeton University Press, 2005), pp. 1–16; and Romand Coles speaks of "the dark ages that threaten us all" in his *Beyond Gated Communities: Reflections for the Possibility of Democracy* (Minneapolis: University of Minnesota Press, 2005), p. xxxvi.

2. Jodi Dean, "The Politics of Avoidance: The Limits of Weak Ontology," p. 58 in "Commitments in a Post-Foundationalist World: Exploring the Possibilities of 'Weak Ontology,' " special issue, *Hedgehog Review* 7:2 (Summer 2005): 58.

3. Sheldon Wolin, *Politics and Vision* (Boston: Little, Brown and Co., 1960); and the second edition (2004) of this book cited in Note 1 of this chapter.

4. Wolin, *Politics and Vision* (1960), chap. 1.

5. Wolin, "Fugitive Democracy," *Constellations* 1:1 (April 1994): 19, 23–24.

6. In the United States, for example, a plausible argument can be made that at least the latter expectation was met to some degree from the late 1940s to the 1970s; that is, during that period, the percentage increase in income experienced by those at the bottom of society was higher than those at the very top. See the American Political Science Association (APSA) Task Force Report, "American Democracy in an Age of Rising Inequality," *Perspectives on Politics* 2:4 (December 2004): 651–666.

7. APSA Task Force Report, "American Democracy." As of the 2008 election campaign, the issue of inequality began to be taken more seriously in national politics.

8. Robert Perrucci and Earl Wysong, *The New Class Society: Goodbye to the American Dream?* (Lanham, Md.: Roman and Littlefield, 2003), chap. 1.

9. On the amount of income inequality in Western democracies, see Lawrence R. Jacobs and Theda Skocpol, eds., *Inequality and American Democracy: What We Know and What We Need to Learn* (New York: Russell Sage Foundation, 2005), pp. 160–162.

10. Although the United States has a "high average income," comparatively speaking, "absolute poverty . . . is much higher . . . than in the other advanced industrialized democracies"; Jacobs and Skocpol, eds., *Inequality and American Democracy*, p. 164.

11. Obviously, what you take as a criterion of real material misery is a matter of debate. One measure might be the number of people in the United States who actually report literally not having enough to eat. That turns out to be about 1 million people out of a population of some 300 million; see Christopher Jencks, "Whatever Happened to Welfare?" *New York Review of Books,* December 15, 2005, p. 79. If we take misery less literally, say, in the sense of needing food stamps, we find that the number is 28 million, or about 10 percent of the population; see Erik Eckholm, "As Jobs Vanish and Prices Rise, Food Stamp Use Nears Record," *New York Times,* March 31, 2008, http://www.nytimes.com/2008/03/31/us/31foodstamps.html?_r=1 &ref=opinion&oref=slogin (accessed 4/15/08). Another measure would be the percentage of people who fall below the official poverty line in the United States or who don't have health insurance; the figure for both these measures is about 15 percent of the population. See John Graves and Sharon K. Long, "Why Do People Lack Health Insurance?" *Urban Institute Report,* May 22, 2006, http://www.urban.org/publications/411317.html (accessed 4/30/08); for the percentage of people who fall below the official poverty line, see the Web page of the U.S. Census Bureau, http://www.census.gov (accessed 4/15/08).

My intention in citing these figures is certainly not to argue that the number of people in these categories is acceptable; rather it is simply to suggest that the idea of a demos composed of those who are materially disadvantaged in a deep sense—Wolin refers to those who are "preoccupied with economic survival"—does not constitute a majority of the citizens in a country such as the United States today. See Wolin, *Politics and Vision* (2004), p. 602.

12. Research on the Netherlands has shown that "anger and resentment" toward immigrant minorities are driven both by cultural or national identity-based concerns and economic interest concerns, although the former is the most significant factor. Additionally, the anti-immigrant feelings are not restricted to the most disadvantaged ("the maladjusted, less educated, and marginal"), but extend into both the middle and upper segments; Paul M. Sniderman, Louk Hagendoorn, and Markus Prior, "Predisposing Factors and Situational Triggers: Exclusionary Reactions to Immigrant Minorities," *American Political Science Review* 98:1 (February 2004): 35–36, 45–46. For evidence from the United States regarding attitudes toward excluding immigrants, see Peter Burns and James G. Gimpel, "Economic Insecurity, Prejudicial Stereotypes, and Public Opinion on Immigration Policy," *Political Science Quarterly* 115: 2 (Summer 2000): 201–225. They also find both economic and identity-based causes.

It should be emphasized here that my claims about resentment and hostility in the middle segment of prosperous Western societies should not be taken as implying that this middle group is the only one expressing such feelings toward social and cultural "others." My point rather is to indicate that the presence of these attitudes in the middle segment becomes particularly problematic today, if one accepts my contention that late-modern democracies are faced with having to appeal to at least some in this middle when constructing strong democratic coalitions.

13. Jürgen Habermas, *Between Facts and Norms*, pp. 135–136, 289–299.

14. Laclau's first survey of these concerns appeared in Laclau and Chantal Mouffe, *Hegemony and Socialist Strategy: Towards a Radical Democratic Politics* (London: Verso, 1985). Laclau not only delegitimizes any ideal of a collective autonomy, he also has the same opinion of any normative concept; that is, it is simply a cover for some group's hegemony. For example, justice is nothing more than a vacant ideal into which the demands of various groups can be projected; see his *On Populist Reason* (London: Verso, 2005) pp. 98–99.

15. Wolin, *Politics and Vision* (2004), preface and chap. 17.

16. Ibid., pp. 582–586.

17. Ibid., p. 603.

18. Ibid.

19. Ibid., pp. 561–562, 568, 578, 586–89.

20. Ibid., pp. 601–602.

21. Ibid., p. 602.

22. Derrida, *Specters of Marx*, pp. 59, 75.

23. Ibid., p. 59; and "On Cosmopolitanism," in *On Cosmopolitanism and Forgiveness*, trans. Mark Dooley and Michael Hughes, preface by Simon Critchley and Richard Kearney (London: Routledge, 2002), p. 23.

24. Derrida, *Specters of Marx*, pp. 25–27.

25. Ibid., pp. 22–23, 28.

26. Ibid., pp. 59, 75.

27. I don't want this point about the abstractness of Derrida's notion of democracy to be misinterpreted. I am certainly not criticizing his actual willingness to undertake political action. Personally, he engaged in an admirable way with many political issues and sometimes let his philosophical insights recommend certain policy stances. See, for example, his advocacy of "cities of refuge" in "On Cosmopolitanism," pp. 3–24.

28. Connolly, *The Ethos of Pluralization*, pp. 180–188.

29. Ibid., pp. xviii, 21, 92, 234; and *Why I Am Not a Secularist* (Minneapolis: University of Minnesota Press, 1999), p. 151.

30. Connolly, *The Ethos of Pluralization*, pp. xviii, 92.

31. Ibid., pp. 93–97.

32. Romand Coles, *Rethinking Generosity*, pp. 191–194.

33. Taylor, *Philosophical Arguments*, p. xii.

34. Connolly, *Ethos of Pluralization*, p. xii.

35. The fact that I am not trying to make a systematic set of arguments against inequality in this context does not preclude such arguments. My intention is to provide some of the basic components from which such arguments could be made.

36. Of course, the economic, rational actor figures prominently in models of politics preferred by many political scientists. For a perceptive treatment of this development in political science, see Mark Petracca, "The Rational Actor Approach to Politics: Science, Self-Interest and Normative Democratic Theory," in *The Economic Approach to Politics: A Critical Reassessment of the Theory of Rational Action*, ed. Kirsten Renwick Monroe (New York: HarperCollins, 1991), pp. 171–203.

37. See, for example, John Noble Wilford, "Almost Human, and Sometimes Smarter," *New York Times*, April 17, 2007, pp. D1.

38. William Connolly, "White Noise," *Hedgehog Review*, 7:2 (Summer 2005): 33.

39. Dean, "The Politics of Avoidance." See also Antonio Vasquez-Arroyo, "Agonized Liberalism: The Liberal Theory of William E. Connolly," *Radical Philosophy* 127 (September/October 2004) p. 10; and Wolin, *Politics and Vision* (2004), pp. 581–584. Wendy Brown both articulates her own idea of an ethos of "civic love" and expresses the worry that the recourse to an ethos may be just a manifestation of despair by the political left; *Edgework*, pp. 22–23, 35–36; and "Democracy and Bad Dreams," *Theory & Event* 10:1 (2007): para. 18.

40. Dean, "The Politics of Avoidance," p. 56; and "Change of Address, in Terrell Carvier and Samuel Chambers, eds., *Judith Butler's Precarious Politics* (London: Routledge, 2008), p. 109.

41. Richard Flathman, interview by Keith Topper, "An Interview with Richard Flathman," *Hedgehog Review* 7:2 (Summer 2005): 106. Cf. Dean, "The Politics of Avoidance," p. 57.

42. The dog illustration was offered in Flathman, "The Bearable Lightness of Being: Weak Ontology and the Affirmation of Moral and Political Life" (Conference

paper, Center for Global Culture and Communication, Northwestern University, Evanston, Ill., March 5-6, 2004).

43. Flathman, "An Interview with Richard Flathman," p. 106.

44. William James, *The Will to Believe and Other Essays in Popular Philosophy* (New York: Cosimo, 2006), pp. 1–31.

45. Dean, "The Politics of Avoidance," pp. 55–56; see also Vasquez-Arroyo, "Agonized Liberalism," pp. 11ff.

46. See, for example, M. Garbar and Rebecca L. Walkowitz, eds., *The Turn to Ethics* (New York: Routledge, 2000); Peter Baker, *Deconstruction and the Ethical Turn* (Gainesville: University Press of Florida, 1995); Todd F. Davis and Kenneth Womack, eds., *Mapping the Ethical Turn: A Reader in Ethics, Culture and Literary Theory* (Charlottesville: University of Virginia Press, 2001); and Amanda Anderson, *The Way We Argue Now*, p. 8ff.

47. Dean, "The Politics of Avoidance," p. 57. Dean's critique of Butler is contained in "Change of Address," pp. 109-126.

48. Dean, "Change of Address," p. 109; and "The Politics of Avoidance," p. 55.

49. Vasquez-Arroyo, "Agonized Liberalism," p. 16.

50. The quotation from President Bush comes from a joint press conference with the French president, Jacques Chirac, at the White House on November 6, 2001.

51. Dean, "The Politics of Avoidance," p. 58.

52. Ibid., p. 56.

53. Levinas might not like my description of his scene of the self and other as an ontological one. For him, it is the original ethical scene that we face before any ontological speculation. I see the ethical and the ontological as equiprimordial.

54. See, for example, Jacques Derrida, "The Force of Law: The 'Mystical Foundation of Authority,'" *Acts of Religion* (New York: Routledge, 2002), pp. 230–298; *Of Hospitality: Anne Dufourmantell Invites Jacques Derrida to Respond* (Stanford, Calif.: Stanford University Press, 2000), pp. 25–27; and "On Cosmopolitanism," pp. 3–23.

55. Louis Althusser, "Ideology and the Ideological State Apparatuses: Notes toward an Investigation," in *Lenin and Philosophy and Other Essays*, trans. B. Brewster (New York: Monthly Review Press, 1971).

56. Judith Butler, *Gender Trouble: Feminism and the Subversion of Identity* (London: Routledge, 1990. In her later work, the basic figuration of self, other, and social norm is constructed in more psychoanalytic terms. This brings ethical-political matters to life in a somewhat different fashion. And, I would argue, a more philosophically powerful one, because the figures she now employs display more clearly the positive ontological animation of Butler's sustained and creative understanding of power. See especially her *Precarious Life.*

57. Habermas, "Wahrheitstheorien," in *Wirklichkeit und Reflexion: Walter Schulz zum 60 Geburtstag,* ed. H. Fahrenbach (Pfullingen: Neske, 1973), pp. 211–263.

58. Habermas, *The Theory of Communicative Action*, vol. I, *Reason and the Rationalization of Society*, trans. Thomas McCarthy (Boston: Beacon Press, 1981), pt. 1, chap. 1, and pt. 3.

59. Ibid., pp. 306–308.

60. Ibid., p. 287; and *The Philosophical Discourse of Modernity: Twelve Lectures*, trans. Frederick Lawrence (Cambridge, Mass.: MIT Press, 1987), p. 311.

61. Besides Rorty, who looks to the criterion of avoiding cruelty, the other major political theorist who pursues a negative approach is Judith Shklar, *The Faces of Injustice* (New Haven, Conn.: Yale University Press, 1990). I made use of this kind of perspective earlier in *Political Theory and Postmodernism*, pp. 122–126.

62. Rorty, *Contingency, Irony and Solidarity*, pp. xvi, 92.

63. Rorty, "Remarks on Deconstruction and Pragmatism," in *Deconstruction and Pragmatism*, p. 17.

64. I elaborate at length upon how such a critical social theory can overcome the dangers Rorty thinks are unavoidable in such claims about power in my "The Very Idea of a Critical Social Science," in *The Cambridge Companion to Critical Theory*, ed. Fred Rush (Cambridge: Cambridge University Press, 2004), pp. 328–330.

6. Conclusion

1. The terminology of *reductio* is borrowed from Jacob Levy, "Liberal Jacobinism," *Ethics* 114 (2004): 334.

2. Wendy Brown, *Regulating Aversion*, p. 88.

3. Ibid. Brown worries (correctly to my mind) about a tolerance that takes identity as given; pp. 88–90.

4. Rorty, *Contingency, Irony and Solidarity*, pp. xv–xvi.

5. Ibid., pp. xii–xiv, 42, 67–68.

6. Ibid., pp. xiv, 80.

7. Ibid., pp. xv, 68, 74, 92–94.

8. Ibid., pp. 88, 94. In Chapter 4, I explored problems that arise from trying to use pain in this foundational fashion.

9. Ibid., pp. 42–43.

10. See my *Sustaining Affirmation*, pp. 16–19, for further reflections on this matter.

11. Nietzsche, *On the Genealogy of Morals*, pp. 18–24.

12. Taylor, *Sources of the Self*, pp. 515–517.

13. Ibid., pp. 211–233.

14. See the editorial by Cal Thomas, "Immigration Woes Revealed," *Daily Progress*, November 30, 2007, p. 8. Thomas is enthusiastically quoting Patrick Buchanan.

15. The televised debate was reported in M. D. Shear and D. Balz, "Romney and Guiliani Clash in GOP's CNN/YouTube Debate," *Washington Post*, November 29, 2007 p. A1.

16. See the group's Web site at http://www.minutemanproject.com (accessed 3/5/08).

17. Coles, *Beyond Gated Politics,* pp. 213–237.

18. "Trekking to Make a Point: Advocacy Group to Walk Immigrants' Path," *Daily Progress,* February 25, 2008, p. 1.

19. Norman L. Zucker and Naomi Flink Zucker, *The Guarded Gate: The Reality of American Refugee Policy* (San Diego: Harcourt Brace Jovanovich, 1987), p. xvii. See also the public opinion survey, "America's Immigration Quandary," sec. 4, "Views and Perceptions of Immigrants," March 30, 2006, http:/www.people-press.org (accessed 12/6/07).

20. Raymond Geuss, *Outside Ethics* (Princeton, N.J.: Princeton University Press, 2005), pp. 38–39.

Index

Harvard University Press is a member of Green Press Initiative (greenpressinitiative.org), a nonprofit organization working to help publishers and printers increase their use of recycled paper and decrease their use of fiber derived from endangered forests. This book was printed on 100% recycled paper containing 50% post-consumer waste and processed chlorine free.